The 4th way

Teaching the Gnostic Wisdom

of

AKIA Philosophy®

Zsa Zsa Tudos

AKIA Publishing

First Edition

Published by AKIA Publishing Copyright © Zsa Zsa Tudos 2018

The author asserts the moral right under the Copyright, Designs and Patents Act 1988 to be identified as the author of this work.

All Rights reserved. No part of this publication may be reproduced, stored in a retrieval system or transmitted, in any form or by any means without the prior consent of the author, nor be otherwise circulated in any form of binding or cover other than that which it is published and without a similar condition being imposed on the subsequent purchaser.

www.zsazsatudos.com

To earthlings

Content

	Page
PROLOGUE	5

Apprentice level – Earth element

1	7
2	21
3	47
4	62

Apprentice level – Spring of Light

1	65
2	78
3	90
4	101
5	115

Healer level – AKIA – HEALING

1	123
2	131
3	144
4	152
5	162
6	172

Healer level – Water element

1	178
2	197
3	227
4	234

PROLOGUE

The whole Universe and everything in it follow a cycle of evolution. As we learn and experience, our frequency gets higher and we become lighter. When I say our, it is not only earthlings but the planet and the Solar system also, to stay near to home. The lighter we are the more difficult it is for us to stay within the magnetic field of Earth. Life becomes unbearable, humanity destroys itself and ends a great cycle. As in every case, destruction is followed by rebuilding and a new cycle begins. However, the motions of the two poles give a degree to the destroying and building. The learned and the more evolved understand the interrelations of energies with the responsibility towards each other and would climb the ladder of evolution by convincing others to create and build together; while lesser individuals would demolish the surroundings to make the peak of their achievement more distinguished and impressive.

When an energy mass is *destroyed* it goes back to the Source, the Creator Force. Logs into the essence of existence and starts building a new one. The physical body of an earthling derives from the ingredients of the planet. The body contains a certain amount of every organic energy traceable in the ground. That is why we recall certain events, thoughts or ideas from thousands of years back. These are fragments of memories focusing on as much as one can take emotionally. To complete the puzzle, a story is created around the idea and announced as true. The attitude of creating a new past works well especially with people of lesser knowledge. These stories dilute reality further and make it quite difficult to find the core in it.

Bearing in mind that the Universe works according to the laws of physics, in the search for the reality, one just has to follow these rules. That is what AKIA Philosophy does.

In my teachings, I use the last cycle of humanity to stay a bit nearer to home. This era is the 5 Sun Ages time that started in around b.c.e. 20.238.

Be patient with your readings! It will all come together in the end. I start with events easiest to comprehend.

On the 28th of December 2012, the events of the Five Sun Ages pushed the whole Galaxy towards a Quantum Leap[1]. It means that the Great Cycle of Humanity has ended.

I am not talking about the Mayan calendar or any other kind of revelation. What we experience doesn't happen because of them, but they remembered the Knowledge and spread the word about forthcoming events. I'd also like to add that the Haya Sophia or Magnum Opus left an identifiable impact on early civilizations.

In this book, I follow certain steps through small workshop units for your convenience.

It is a book, you need to read more than once to understand the core.

Happy thinking!

---

[1] Quantum Leap is an evolutionary move when the entity is taken on the next level of understanding.

AKIA PHILOSOPHY®

APPRENTICE LEVEL

EARTH INITIATION

1

- **Migration**

During the time of Jupiter, at the end of the 1st Sun Age, the Great Deluge made considerable changes at certain points of the planet. Atlantis was cracked and shifted, triggering the migration towards the very centre of the dry land, The Giza plateau in Khem[2]. Members of the procession encoded the secrets of the unseen soul and cosmic knowledge into the soil, the water, the air and the buildings, in order to trigger the mind of future generations. Schools were set up to teach The Knowledge. Other concentrated wisdom carriers are the 13 crystal skulls, organic energies like stones and trees, giving importance to life.

Energy centres such as the Carpathian Basin as the Old Crown and the present Base chakra received a large dose of the Wisdom. It continued with Greece and arrived at the plateau between the Great Rivers of Euphrates and Tigress. Here the people we remember as Sumerians put everything into practice that is spread and still remembered all over the planet.

The Knowledge I am talking about is the Genesis of Keta and that of the Universe. Keta is the ancient name of Earth. It carries the *"everything is interrelated"* and the *"as above so below"* idea.

The Universe is made of numbers. These numbers represent certain data that I call knowledge. The data is energy in the sense of physics therefore it has speed, frequency, colour, sound, taste, substance and fragrance. It also has polarity that

---

[2] Khem – the Land of the Black Soil – is the ancient name for Egypt. Alchemy is Al Khemi that means the Matter of Egypt.

is either + or -. The latter is not the mirror of right or wrong and good or bad. The two polarities keep the organic energy alive by producing different effects and responses to happenings. This motion travels on a spiral.

This spiral is created by the cycles of events. Every event has a beginning and an end. This is a cycle. However, every end is a beginning of another event and middle to yet another. There are bigger cycles and also smaller ones, depending on one's point of view but in the case of energies, they are equally important. As we move forward our deeds and way of thinking are the result of experiences in the past and they create the foundation of the future.

Let me put this train of thoughts into an example. Every day you go through some sort of routine. Only look at the cycle of leaving the house and coming back. You usually take the same route every day, thinking that it would not have changed in your absence. But it would. You can never travel the same road even if you are the only one using it because everything is in motion and changing. By the afternoon, you are not the person you were in the morning and the place you arrive back to is different from the one you left behind earlier. Since you went through certain effects during the day it is added to the cycle of your household. At the end of each cycle, there is a quantum leap. The more important the cycle the bigger the quantum leap.

A year of your life is a cycle. On your birthday in theory, you arrive back to the same day when you were born. Each of these cycles ends on a certain note. The degree of the note depends on your achievements of the year behind. You might close the year on a high note or a low key, and it might just be somewhere in the middle depending mainly on your efforts and openness. Since those cycles operate within your comfort zone, I call them microcosmic cycles. However, there always is some contribution from the Universe that we usually refer to as fate for it is unchangeable. These moves are provided by the interrelation of the micro and macrocosm.

The macrocosm has its own cycles. Let us look at those ruling our lives. Closest to us are the Sun and the Moon cycles. As the 3 + 1 are the key numbers in the Universe, there are 4 Moon cycles. There are also 4 cycles of the 2 together, such as the 2 Equinoxes[3] and the 2 Solstices[4]. A much bigger cycle for earthlings is the Precession of the Equinox[5] which takes about 2,160 years of the common calendar.

The Sun Age is a cycle of the Solar system that takes between 4.000 – 5.200 years depending on the effects of the travel. Four of those would align us with the 4 elements and the fifth is the connection with the Creator force that is the Core, the Essence

---

[3] Equinox is the time when the Sun and the Moon take equal time on Earth. It happens at the end of March or beginning of April and the end of September or beginning of October. The Equinox is the balance of the Moon and Sun therefore it can only happen on the Full Moon.
[4] Solstice is the day when the Sun and consequently the Moon stay with us the longest of the solar year. It usually happens on the end of December or the beginning of January and the end of June or the beginning of July. Solstices also happen on the Full Moon.
[5] Precession of the Equinox is the result of the slight shift between the ruling planets – with the 12-star formations zodiac when in alignment – and the ecliptic. As Earth travels on the ecliptic, it arrives into the court of a planet from the Solar system and earlier under the jurisdiction of a star formation. The permanent point is the Spring Equinox. The mishap is that Earth cannot complete a whole circle around the Sun during the cycle between 2 Spring Equinoxes, therefore it slips back one planet every 2,160 years.

of the ever-expanding Universe. The first Knowledge was able to multiply by division.

In February 2003 C.E. (Common Era) the Neptune energy charged with Pisces was chased out by the newcomer Uranus energy and the New Age started. Most Earthlings would call it the Age of Aquarius; however astronomical changes and our behaviour pattern reshuffled the Solar System and slowed Earth down. As it happened the ecliptic of the planet shortened and moved out of alignment with the 12-star formations zodiac. The effects of the ruling planets are still strongly with us, that is why we call it the Age of Uranus now.

Uranus energy is a much faster and more emotionally charged surrounding than that of Neptune and Pisces. It provided a welcome boost for the quantum leap and speeded up the consciousness of the Golden Era. By the changes in the surrounding, we were pressured to implement certain alterations in our behaviour pattern and way of thinking to get into alignment with the Macrocosm. In order to achieve this, first we need to raise the consciousness of the Microcosm, meaning the Self and Earth. The base of this consciousness for Earthlings is the Initiation sequel of the 4 elements. Initiations – also referred to as Attunements – are available for every Earthling regardless their social background, race, gender, age and religion. It is a deep learning and self-discovering procedure, when the candidate gets into alignment with the element by removing the hindering factors, and opens the possibilities of widening the horizon. The workshop also gives you guidance on how to implement the collected information into everyday living and turn it into wisdom. I think I should mention it here that learning is reminding us of the knowledge we all possess.

Number 4 is the symbol of the 4 basic elements – Earth, Water, Air and Fire – the 4 directions, the Moon cycle of 4 x 7, the 4 sides of the pyramid and it also represents the total consciousness. Everything in the Universe has been created with this number. It is Law, Truth, Order and Realization. The number depicts the Creator – the first knowledge that was able to multiply by division – and its 4 basics naturalistic such as Omnipresence, Wisdom, Love and Immortality.

- **The 4 levels of Initiation**

An Earthling initially has 4 ties to the Universe. By understanding them one by one, the ties are cut to enable the Earthling to gain the ultimate freedom he needs to become an equal part of the Universe. The first of these connections is between the physical body and the planet. It is the whole physical existence. The second is the emotional field that is connected to earthly life. The third is the connection between the Universe and physical existence. The highest level is the fourth when the earthling becomes one with the Universe.

Earthlings are classified according to their Initiation level. The lowest is at the Hylic level. These Earthlings are connected to the material plane and have no connections with a higher level. The next would be those who understand that emotions are the fuel of life machinery and they can only grow through them. This is the Psychic level. The next is the Spiritual level that understands the interrelations of the Micro and Macrocosm.

The fourth and highest is with the astral plane when the total connection with the Universe is made.

It might not be apparent but a large percentage of the population is looking for something to hang onto, something to understand and something to achieve. The problem is the **something** here. Without giving it meaning something is nothing. Those who managed to put aim into the search usually belong to one of the 3 categories. These 3 categories best described by P. D. Ouspensky in his book called *In search of the miraculous*. He is quoting the answer of his teacher, G. Gurdjieff, when he was asking about the ways men acquire immortality. Here is his answer:

"All existing and generally known ways to immortality can be divided into three categories:

1. The way of the fakir.

2. The way of the monk.

3. The way of the yogi."

I find his clarity fascinating. For me, these ways correspond with my teachings on the 3 earthly elements.

There are many meanings to the word FAKIR. I pick out the one that describes a man who uses his physical body to withstand pain. He lies on a bed of nails, swallows fire, cuts himself, and so on. This person conquers his physical plane. He represents earthlings who rule the materia. For them, only the material world exists, without emotions and curiosity about the unknown. Money, possessions and physical enjoyments. They go to the gym, chase financial welfare, eat a lot and make love without feelings. They only believe what they see and go through life with a strong attachment to the planet. At some point in their lives, they usually develop kidney problems or illnesses related to the sexual organs. These people denounce all but the Hylic level of living. To understand your connection to the planet, your body and the materia you need the Earth initiation.

The second way is that of the monks. They give up earthly living, all materials and the pleasures of the physical body to conquer their emotions. They live at the Psychic level. To understand your emotions and the way to deal with them one needs Water initiation.

The third way is that of the yogi. These people work through the mind to connect to the macrocosm. They denounce life as it is with the material and emotions. They live the Spiritual level. To understand the connection and master it you need the Air initiation.

The fourth way is the living and learning way. This is the complete way. When you understand all three elements and with the knowledge gained you aim for the fourth, the Fire of the macrocosm. In order to get there, you have to LIVE LIFE. You can only do that if you comprehend all three ways. The material is conquered, meaning that you grow responsible for your own living, pay your bills and create good living conditions. You also need to be brave to allow your emotions to flow, not to be afraid of their effects. On top of all, you need to open your microcosm. Learn your own self, understand the motion and the interrelations of events. This is the road of an earthling.

However, this road cannot be taken alone. You need a teacher to guide you, lift you up when you fall and push you ahead.

In order to understand the importance of the initiations, we need to talk about the meeting of the 2 triangles.

- **The cross and the meeting of the 2 triangles**

If we want to classify ancient symbols, the simple equal legged cross and the two equilateral triangles slipped into each other are the oldest. They have been with us since The Descend to Atlantis. They are very similar in meanings. In the cross the importance of Earthly living and the soul evolutionary directions are symbolized. The cross also depicts a soul living on Earth, with the choices he has, and the possibilities of making the wrong ones. And yes, the cross also means suffering, for experiences needed to fulfil the task of being; while the 2 triangles stand for the same in basics. However, adding the importance of togetherness, the connection of the Micro and Macrocosm[6], the "*As above so below*"[7] theory. In total, they have the answers to all the questions of our everyday and Universal life.

As every subject this one is a mouthful too, for everything is interrelated. I try to grab it at the most obvious spot. Therefore, I thought, I would start with the 3 as number. First of all, we need to understand, that the Universe is made up of numbers.

---

[6] The microcosm is the place where one feels comfortable in. We might call it the comfort zone. Everything else belongs to the macrocosm. As one's microcosm expands the macrocosm shrinks.
[7] It is an ancient understanding of the interrelations of energies made famous by Hermes Trismegistos, the 3 times Great and Knowledgeable.

Out of all the 10 real numbers - 0 to 9 - the 3 is the most important. There are two sets of three: one down on Earth and one above in the Heavens. The three is the symbol of the whole, the perfect blend of the 2 poles and the essence of living.

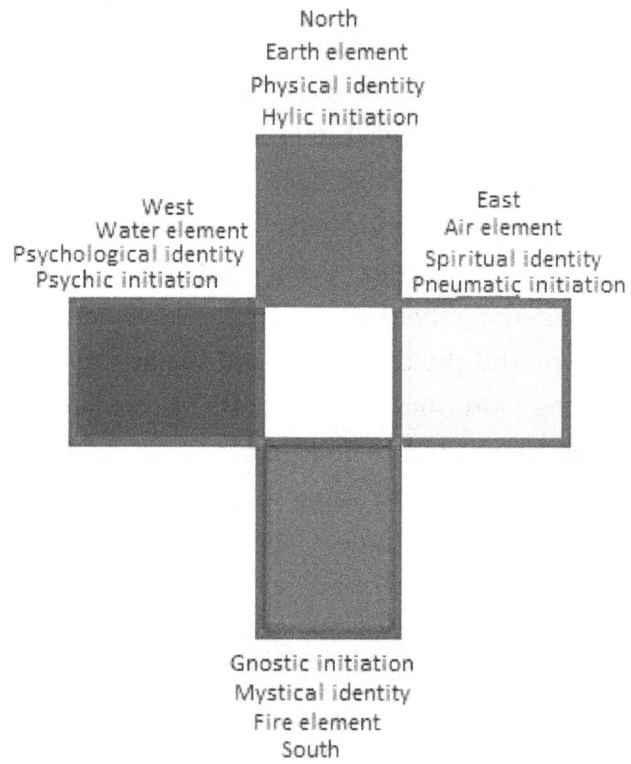

The meeting points of the triangles would show the growth you have achieved.

In Pagan[8] and Shamanic[9] movements, the 3 angles are the man, the woman and the child. The child is the connection between the 2 poles. The 2 genders and the child are symbols here. In our minds they have usually depicted as the smallest nucleus of the family; however, the actual meaning of the scene carries a deeper understanding of human life. The male is representing the Earth energy, for males are usually more earthbound than females. They are more traditional, listen to the conscious more, and have more boundaries. While the female represents the Water energy, being more emotional, letting the subconscious out of the bottle and their boundaries are mobile. To carry on with the thought we arrive at the child. It represents the Air element, for it is still innocent of earth-bounding thought forms, traditions and layers of unnecessary education.

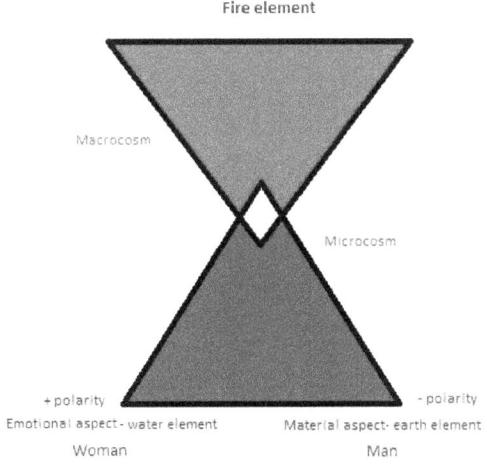

---

[8] Pagan is the Earthling who respects and understands the rules and regulations of nature and lives accordingly.
[9] Shaman is a Shah man, a great healer, knower of herbs and cosmology.

It has the third eye open, capable of channelling, almost a clairvoyant, seeing and understanding the macro and the microcosm. It is connected to the Creator force and by the physical body the connection to Earth is secured. This is the energy that every earthling should become, and also the highest level, every earthling can become. I do not mean that one should preserve the innocence of a child, but one should arrive at an understanding of this energy. 3 is the number of understanding and love - for it is neutral - and it is usually depicted as an equilateral or perfect triangle.

THANKSGIVING MEDITATION

- **The importance of thanksgiving**

The motion has been with us from the beginning as the festivity after the harvest. It is the re-creation of the Pagan festival we usually refer to as Mabon. Like all the other Pagan festivals, Mabon is used by Christianity for religious purposes.

As Spirituality[10] is gaining more and more space therefore the motion of thanksgiving became an everyday practice to make us remember to humble ourselves in front of the greatness and power of the Creator Force.

---

[10] Spirituality is the path to reach and become one with the Creator Force.

The meditation - Thanksgiving

Light one basic white candle and incense. The candle has to be scentless, white and without the metal holder. The incense can be any kind of burning stick, sage or frankincense. It is not advisable to use any other type of so-called purifier, because they are coded for different scenarios and approaches. Stick to tools mentioned in your learning material.

Sit down comfortably with your back straightened and feet on the ground. Imagine a golden beam of Universal Light to descend on the top of your head. Open your head and let the Light in. As you inhale the Light descends further down into your body until it reaches the end of the bone between your ribs. This is the place people usually call 'the gut'. Now imagine that the Light finds its way to flow out of your body at that point where it draws a golden path, the yellow brick road into the infinite distance. You start walking on this road. Do not be afraid of anything and anybody. Remember, you are within yourself so if you meet anybody or see anything they are messages from yourself to you. Pay attention!

You see a meadow in the distance. Walk through it, until you arrive at a dwelling of some kind: it could be a castle or a hut. Open the door and step in. Greet whoever is there. Ask questions from the being(s). If you cannot see anything you can sit around and wait. In case nothing happens, you start saying thanks to whoever you feel comfortable with. You say thanks for things you feel grateful for.

When finished, say farewell and step out of the place. Close the door behind you and start walking back on the same road you came. When you reach 'yourself' pull the Light back into your body, let it flow out of your head and release it into the Universe. Say thanks for the Light.

Warning! It is very important that you follow meditations to the letter to avoid mishaps. If you feel strange after doing one, please get in touch with us on

zsazsa@ex-files.org

After each meditation, you need to write your experiences into your Journal of Journeys.

You may do this meditation as many times as you wish. It would help to clear your vision and sharpen your senses.

As a channel, I designed an encoded sticker with our logo. You might put it anywhere in your house. It could be hidden or seen, doesn't matter. Through this sticker, you'll be part of our healing circle and protection.

Disclaimer

Your address is safe with us and only be used for inevitable connection making. We do not send you letters about our or anybody else's business nor we contact you with personal matters.

AKIA PHILOSOPHY®

APPRENTICE LEVEL

EARTH INITIATION

2

- **Energy centres or chakras**

Everything is energy in the Universe in a true physical sense. It has a sound, a taste, a smell, a substance and a colour to feed vital information to our senses and enable us to understand the other energy. The sharper your senses the clearer information you are getting from the world around. That is what we call chemistry. People with partial senses such as lack of hearing, seeing, smelling and so on, shift the work of the missing sense on the others. That is why blind people would be able to understand more by touching, than others with the 2 senses combined. It is actually the beauty of nature. Everything works for the one, the Whole.

All different energies in the Universe are either organic or non-organic, depending on the state the energy is in. Since everything comes from the Creator Source, all the energies are organic at the beginning. Some become non-organic later by the interference of other energies such as mankind.

Organic energies are constantly changing, therefore evolving. They are living substances. Non-organic energies are much slower in changing and they only take the path of deteriorations; until one day arrive at the point when in a new consciousness, they reborn as an organic energy to get into the never-ending cycle of life again.

Example: a table is made of organic energies like wood and minerals that have been processed into a non-organic, dormant state. Depending on the manufacturing, after some times this energy matrix falls apart and becomes one with the organic energy cycle. It might experience different stages through manufacturing or we might refer to it as recycling before arriving to the *quantum leap* of changing status from non-organic to organic. However, it is the time when the energy particles lose their connection with each other and totally fall apart in order to come alive in a different blend. It is the best example of alchemy in Nature with an unfortunate interference by Earthlings.

We usually think of energy as something that cannot be seen or felt. It is not true. No energy particle exists on its own. They form a group and circle around a magnetic leader quality cell. The stronger the pull the denser the energy would become. The denser the energy the easier is to see it with the physical eye. It is because we only see the reflection of the light and not the object itself. And it happens only if light cannot travel through the object.

These energy circles are connected and interrelated by energy lines. These lines form the matrix of the energy mass. Where 2 lines meet they form an energy centre we usually refer to as chakra from Sanskrit, the language of Far-Eastern philosophies and religions such as Hinduism and Buddhism. There are smaller and bigger centres depending on the number of the crossing energy lines.

Due to the meeting lines, energy centres work like roundabouts; a vortex-like motion is created. This motion and the size of the roundabout is the result of the number of lines meeting at every given place. Small chakras are used by acupuncture, the bigger are good for meridian healing, and the largest ones are places for psychological, physical and astral modifications.

Non-organic energies do not have a specific number of chakras; it varies according to the nature of the energy mass. However, it means that even though a table is non-organic it still has energy centres. In our practices, we use them for altering the behaviour pattern of the object.

Practice

All non-organic energies have an organic past. Face your palm down and hover it over objects without touching. Feel the energy. You'll find that there are denser and thinner points according to the interrelation of energy lines. Hold your hand over the heavy points. Open your mind and let the information come to you about the object. With a lot of practice, you will be able to see the forest where the wood originates from, read the lives of the workers, see the manufacturers, the logistic company and the store you bought your table from.

Observe yourself in stores like IKEA where there are many samples of the same product. They look the same, coloured the same and built the same. However, you always like one the best. Think about the feeling you receive from it. If you let it, the whole life story of the furniture would come to you including the family lives of the workers in the production.

Organic energies have 7 major chakras through which the exchange of energy is conducted. Each of these centres is connected to a major organ. Every thought form related to the energy centre affects this organ first of all. That is why people suffering from depression usually have kidney problems, worries would sit on your digestive system and people with bitterness will develop gall bladder related diseases.

In the case of Earthlings these centres are as follows:

1.

Base or root chakra is situated behind the caudal vertebra at the base of the spine. It holds the spine, takes care of the kidneys; all the feelings related to permanence would settle down here.

BRIEF ANALYSIS

This is the only chakra to stays where it has always been to hold the spine and keep us connected to Earth. In the ever-changing existence, this permanence puts a lot of strain on the energy centre that is visible even to untrained eyes. More and more children are born with bad body structures and bent spines. When I look at youngsters walking on the street my heart weeps; a great majority of them have no idea how to carry themselves and nobody seems to care. We take basic body functions like walking for granted thinking that it comes naturally. However, only the *"what to do"* is natural not the *"how to do"* it. It is due to the fashion with which we bring up our children nowadays or should I say do not bring up our children nowadays. It is a fashionable movement that children should bring up themselves to allow them to develop the way they feel fit rather than give guidance. As I mentioned before, nothing happens in vain. Children are new souls with fast high-frequency energies. Most of them are volunteers and came down here to take part in this extraordinarily exciting time of changes we are very lucky to experience. Since they do not carry karma, their knowledge is intact and near the surface. They bear a good connection to the macrocosm however they do not understand earthly living whatsoever. The guidance they are looking for doesn't arrive therefore frustration and insecurity set in and the struggle to find a balance pushes them towards arrogance, despair, insecurity, carelessness and on many occasions, depression. These are all starting points for drugs, alcohol abuse and suicidal behaviour. On the other hand, parents are new souls also and the guidance they received from their parents are not fit for the new souls for it embraces old moral systems, inbuilt fear and false pride. Apart from having a bent or a curved spine in many cases they develop kidney problems. As the organ responsible for ties and connections to the material and fellow human beings, kidneys go through a lot for the growing insecurity brings a tighter grip on belongings. I'd like to remind you here that security is an illusion and to pursue it is a waste of time and effort.

2.

Sex chakra is in the navel now. It looks after the reproductive organs and sex related feelings.

BRIEF ANALYSIS

Due to strong religious influences and confusion about sexuality, this is the most delicate chakra and the hardest to analyse. It is the true mirror of the human being. It tells you everything related to the earthling, its physical, mental and emotional state, its past, present and future, its behaviour pattern and beliefs. I do my best to unfold this energy centre for you without being very forward. The first thought form we need to get familiar with is that sexual energy is the highest frequency energy a human being has access to. It is the elixir of life and the cradle of light. The next important thought is that sex is not the intercourse but it is in everything. It is the ultimate openness, total surrender and deepest experience. One can only be totally happy and open for development if one's relationship with sexuality is right. Nowadays it is very hard to establish an unconditional connection to sex. To look at it as the spring of light and not the greatest sin is a huge turning point that is hardened by a lack of proper education. When I mention sexual education, I am not thinking of the function of the reproductive system. I am talking about the way to discover the ecstatic beauty in nature and life. However, in everyday life not understanding the essence of the art is the base of every kind of relationship. Sons prefer their mothers and daughters get on better with their fathers. Mothers tend to look after their sons and keep them at home long after becoming an adult. When the daughter stays at home, she is the one who looks after the mother. Girls use their fathers as raw models either way when it comes to choosing someone for partnership and boys would look for somebody resembling their mother in behaviour pattern. On the other hand, when a son is born the mother forms attachment with the new male in the house and slowly detaches herself from the partner who is usually the father of the child. She would seek the affection of the son, would live according to his requirements and follow his opinion. The father would usually turn away from the mother and put the daughter on a pedestal. I need not say how much sorrow, pain and unhappiness comes from this behaviour pattern. It slowly eats you away and makes you forget about the real task in life, - your happiness and your individual aims. There are certain misunderstandings we need to clear up. Although we use the expression, we are planning a family or do you have a family when referring to children, the word means a certain unit of individuals who help each other to maintain their existence and to reach fulfilment. One should never hope for happiness through somebody else and putting this responsibility on your children is selfish for with this attachment you halt the course of your own life and put a great strain on your children. At a later stage when you recognize your losses it is too late to alter the situation. Then again nothing is ever too late. You cannot change the past. However, with the experience gained you could plan a much better future for yourself. This is the energy centre where detachment is formed and one learns the essence of the unconditional love, we are willing to talk about even though understanding doesn't accompany these words. Without grasping the fact that peace, happiness and fulfilment can only be established within and for that, you are the sole responsible, life would never bring what you desire.

3.

Solar plexus is 2 palm widths above the navel. It is to keep the body in balance and to look after the stomach, the gall bladder, the liver pancreas and the nervous system. Feelings related to humanity at large settle here.

BRIEF ANALYSIS

The digestive system is the most complex chemical plant that has ever been created. It is set to digest all kinds of organic energies. However, non-organic food would make permanent residues in the large intestines and alter the work of the factory. It is getting harder to keep the system working properly for we use a lot of artificial ingredients in our food especially in the most popular fast food products and the beloved Coca-Cola. Food as the largest conscious energy intake should be under scrutiny. There is a lot for responsible earthlings to consider especially if they want to stay in alignment with their own energy field. Here I would greatly recommend my book titled Energies on the table, available worldwide, that talks about eating in the spiritual way. However, it is not only food that uses the digestive system. All your thoughts about the world, politics, work, media, and so on, go through the machinery of digestion. This is all well, however, the problem starts when earthlings keep energies in the digestive system for longer than necessary and continue chewing on thoughts and events. The longer it goes on, the greater the damage is, for this chemical plant doesn't make a difference between impulses and actual food and the enzyme production keeps on. As a consequence, the body starts chewing on itself and in most cases, it results in physical discomfort and later disease. Language mirrors this view by stating that a particular human being is eaten up by sorrow or worry. In this case, the feelings are displayed for everybody to see and generously added to the basket of energies we share. I call this the martyr syndrome for a painful sacrifice is made in order to alter the life of others. It might be a very popular behaviour pattern nowadays but its true meaning is very far from the fashionable idea we nurture. There are others who keep things private and instead of exhibiting their pain and it builds a safety belt around the waist and belly. The advantage of this behaviour is that the slow energy is not there to share. That is probably why overweight people are happier. It is naive to believe that one could be redeemed by someone else's suffering. One cannot learn from the experience of others for it would never become knowledge. Also, important to understand is that sacrifice is a choice of the being with the responsibility comes with it. Since it doesn't spread joy or happiness - only sorrow and guilt - the accountability is vast. There is always a selfish thought behind sacrifice. Either you are a victim of a painful existence or you actually inflict the pain on someone else, the result is the same. You are pushing your views into the limelight forcing people to follow your opinion. To make the whole impact worse it usually happens in the name of love and care. And we still call love unconditional. I think I need to add an important thought here: it is impossible to live up to the expectations of others unless you are in a closed community where everything happens according to set rules and regulations. There is always going to be somebody who does not particularly like you or talks against you. Tolerance and forgiveness are good companions in these moments and bear in mind that earthlings perform 100% of their abilities at every given moment.

4.

Heart chakra is a palm width above the solar plexus. It is responsible for the heart, blood circulation and the vagus nerve. Strong and shocking feelings affect this chakra.

BRIEF ANALYSIS

Although the widely-recognized belief is that feelings come from the heart it really has very little to do with it. The only feelings landing here come through the vagus nerve which is actually in the throat. Sudden and unexpected events affect it hence why we say my heart is in my throat. Spiritually long term or permanent slow energy feelings take up residents in the heart, especially a loss of any kind. I'd like to mention here that I find it very sad and also funny that we never hang onto anything happy. It is due to the slow energies of the Pisces era that put a gap between the 2 triangles and doomed earthlings to unhappiness. Fortunately, this deed is self-inflicted from the microcosm; the Universe has never given up on us.

5.

Throat chakra is in the mouth. Its job is to take care of the bronchial and vocal system, the lungs and the alimentary canal. Problems related to willpower, responsibility, dreams and communication show at this chakra.

BRIEF ANALYSIS

Everything arriving at the throat chakra goes through the thyroid gland which acts as a go-between thought forms and the body, making up the neutral part of the trinity structure that is in everything. As a reminder trinity of the Universal structure has nothing to do with any form of religion, it is the 2 poles of the positive and negative polarity and the neutral connection. However religious movements adopted and altered this form to fit their own understanding of the Universe and still use it as the base for their rules and regulations. Bear in mind also that positive and negative are not fit to substitute good or bad in any way whatsoever; they are the two poles present in every segment, the mirror effects that trigger the motion of existence. The thyroid gland acts as the interpreter between thought forms and the physical part of the body. As a go-between it strives to be impartial, truthfully translating impulses and thoughts into chemicals to make them understandable for the body; on the other hand, chemical reactions from the body become impulses to make it comprehensible for the brain. The work of the interpreter is very important indeed. It has to be fit and fully functional to deliver the work. However, this duty puts a lot of strain on the organ and in many cases the stress causes malfunctioning. It happens when mass production of thoughts flood, the thyroid in an unorganized manner seeking translation all at once. I am certain it sounds intriguing however, thought-forms are organic energies as I am going to talk about them a bit later on in the book. Apart from thoughts the throat chakra also takes in feelings connected to responsibilities, unfulfilled dreams and wishes, communication skills and willpower. Without responsibilities, life doesn't exist. Basically, one is responsible for every effect one puts on the Universe which one constantly does. Although an unspoken responsibility, it is the most effective contribution towards the Whole that earthlings are part of. Dreams and wishes play an important role in the wellbeing of the Throat Chakra for earthlings seem to have many but act on few. From childhood, ideas about life, dreams about certain professions and lifestyles accumulate in the throat and turn into residues once being neglected for a certain period of time. Earthlings grow up fed on the media from a tender age and their wishes and dreams about adulthood would come from the same source. These dreams are usually shattered when they get to the stage of action for reality is nothing like fairy tales. It is all very well to watch films and read stories with the understanding that they are subjective views of other earthlings. Even history is written by someone who wasn't an active partaker and looks at events from a personal point of view. However, in most cases, this guidance is missing and dreams remain in the comfortable dwelling of the Throat Chakra. Since it is the bridge with a 2 ways road it affects both the physical and the spiritual bodies, meaning the conscious and the subconscious therefore this residue is a real poison.

With my students, we practice making inventories or taking stocks twice a year. We usually do them around the solstices because they proved to have favourable energies for it. I give you the recipe here.

- **Stock Taking**

Take 4 sheets of A4 size papers. On the first write everything you love about yourself – interior and exterior. On the second you write things you do not love in yourself – interior and exterior. It is very important to be honest. Your writing shouldn't mirror the opinion of your surroundings or the mass consciousness but your own feelings about yourself. Bear in mind that everybody is beautiful and ugly, good and bad and so on. These are subjective opinions brushing the surface rather than giving thorough accounts. You might arrive at the conclusion that you do not know. Well, then it is time to get to know yourself. How can you know about the world if you do not know who you are? Look into the mirror and observe. Watch your deeds and thoughts. Be flexible with your writing! You can add and remove as you feel. Do it for about 4 weeks and then look at the result. You might have put down certain unchangeable dislikes, such as you are short, tall, brown-eyed, overweight, skinny, and so on. Well, whatever you do you cannot become taller or shorter. It is a genetic inheritance you have to live with. The colour of your hair or eyes can be altered easily. If they bother you so much get on with it and change them. However, the rest should be accepted and loved for they are the part of you. Eventually, everything should disappear from the dislike page. To live with hatred towards the self is a very dangerous ground for a happy existence. The third paper should contain all your dreams since childhood and on the fourth, you note down the ones that became a reality - whether they were helped by the natural course of life or a result of your conscious work. Children are usually hooked on certain characters for their extraordinary abilities, fame, beauty or pretty uniforms. Becoming a prima ballerina, actor, pop-star, superman, pilot, conductor and soldier are amongst their dreams for the future. You might think they are not important anymore for time has put a solution to these dreams. This is a laid-back approach for time doesn't heal it only pushes thoughts and feelings into the background. It works like a wardrobe. You buy a new pullover that you put in a visible place to give yourself the pleasure of looking at it. As time passes you use and wash and place it back in the front. Only when you suddenly have the idea of reorganizing your wardrobe you find that many nice jumpers are in the back and many are ready to be given away. As you go through your wardrobe you remember the events attached that you need to sort out. By doing it you achieve closure on the past. The very same procedure applies to dreams. Going through them you are able to close certain chapters and change thought forms in your life. Be aware that people always give what they are capable of therefore you need to stop blaming others for events in your life. Your parents didn't enrol you in ballet school or singing lessons because their way of looking at life, and the picture they formed about your future didn't allow it. As a grown-up to become a prima-ballerina is not an option any longer. However, singing is still an open avenue for you to pursue. Take it up and make the most of your life.

6.

Forehead chakra is at the hairline or where it used to be. It looks after the nervous system, the left eye, the lower brain, the nose and ears.

BRIEF ANALYSIS

This is the place where everything happens. It is the meeting point of the 3 bodies – the astral, the spiritual and the physical – where thoughts and experiences are exchanged. It is the bridge between the conscious and the subconscious. Furthermore, it is the place where the macrocosmic triangle touches the microcosmic one and if circumstances permit, they start slipping into each other. This action is controlled by the trinity of the eyes. The left eye is the Water, subconscious and positive; the right is the Earth, conscious and negative in polarity; and the third eye is the neutral one, keeping the balance between the two planes. It is the place where Knowledge flows in attached to the Light as the conveyor of cosmic experiences. This is the result of a very complex information exchange brought in by the senses. As I mentioned earlier, we only focus on one eye at every given time according to the initial viewpoint we stored in the brain. Using the right eye, we would be looking for a so-called realistic view while the left gives us some room for improvement. However, regardless of which eye we use the information received would end up in two places at the same time: in the subconscious and the conscious.

The third eye or the neutral eye is called by different names to fit the philosophy or religion: God's eye, the eye that sees everything or it is preceded by the name of a certain prophet. I like the idea of ancient Egypt and usually call it the Eye of Horus for it fits the trinity structure of the Universe: Isis, Osiris and Horus. Also, the Eye of Horus, like everything else from the same place is designed according to the function of the pathway. Therefore, the eye has 6 doors. They are assigned to the senses where impulses and information come in. It mirrors the evolutionary state of the soul with the hindering and forwarding behaviour patterns and thought-forms.

Remember that everything is energy for everything carries knowledge. The Eye of Horus mirrors the way we use our senses:

The whole eye is 1 hequat by ancient Egyptian measurement that is depicted as a mouth for it is one bite: the biggest and the smallest segment. It is also the physical gate between the macro and microcosms. While on Earth spiritual and physical nourishment arrives through it; on departure, the soul leaves the body here. One hequat is 320 ro.

1. In the right lower corner of the eye there is a twig which we put into the ground to grow vegetables. It is a connection to the planet and is the gate of touching. Out of the 320 ro touching would take up 5 - that is 1/64th of the whole.

2. The curved line going towards the left lower corner symbolizes the wheat when it is budding. The wheat is the food we put into our mouths. It is the taste. Taste is actually touch and forms, meaning that we taste by touching different forms. This view puts tasting in front of touching and assigns 10 ro to the sense - 1/32nd of the whole.

3. The left corner of the eye is the nearest to the ear. It has the shape of a horn. Through this instrument, the sound is tasted and touched. Therefore, hearing is the sum of touching and tasting. 20 ro are assigned to it - it is 1/16th of the whole.

4. We do not actually talk about thoughts as one of the senses, however, they are very important. The long line above the eye represents the thoughts for we use our eyebrow to mirror our thoughts. They are considered to be the sum of touching,

tasting and hearing. A thought is a silent voice. 40 ro are assigned to it; that is 1/8th of the whole.

5. The circle in the middle represents the actual eye. Seeing is the sum of tasting, touching, hearing and thinking. It receives 80 ro - to take up 1/4th of the whole. The horizon has no ends just like a spiral. Do not forget, the circle is a 2-dimensional spiral. As long as we see it as a circle there are limits to it. We create limits.

6. The smelling is symbolized by the triangle nearest the nose. It is everything together. 160 ro are assigned to this sense - it takes up ½ of the whole. Our senses have been distorted by ideas and belief systems. Fear prevents earthlings from using the gateways correctly. The notion I believe it when I see it puts a hold on spiritual education for seeing is an illusion as we only see the mirrored light and what we allow ourselves to take in.

7.

Crown chakra is located about 10 cm above the head. It looks after the upper brain and the right eye.

BRIEF ANALYSIS

In this chakra there is the institution called the Mind. Information and impulses arriving through the forehead centre are sent here for further consideration. These are added to the already existing files or folders and then particular understandings and viewpoints are changed.

In everyday life, Earthlings go through traumas, mishaps, joy, happiness, pleasure, hatred, envy, devilishness, fear, sadness, pain, love and other controversial emotions. Not many of us understand that all our deeds and feelings actually spring from the mind. The Mind is a management centre, where a worker or workers - depending on the size of the company - process the data stored in the filing cabinet, called Brain. Some of the various folders are labelled as Past Lives, Present, Future, Soul Siblings, Tasks, while others are waiting to be organized. These are part of the subconscious, ready to be discovered and used as part of the knowledge, the wisdom that helps us with our endeavours on the path to becoming better human beings in the sense of unity and wholeness. Other ones, like Dwelling, Work, Money, Car, Education, Holiday, Relationship and other effects, are neatly filed into the very front of the cabinet for easy access. The largest of them all has Miscellaneous scribbled on the front with an indescribable hue of pink. It stores runaway files that sort of limber undecidedly between the conscience and the subconscious existing.

As an example, let us look at the first folder entitled Past Lives. It stores the data of one's ancestors, the soul-number, the basic abilities – so-called codes - works the soul accomplished, events it passed through, experiences it had, battles it conquered or lost, and most importantly the knowledge the soul collected during its lives prior to the one it struggles with or enjoys here, down on this wonderful planet called Earth. To be able to understand the purpose of these files, their interrelations and effects on every moment of living, we need to define certain things we keep talking about. The most important is to mention again that in the Universe everything is energy in the physical sense. As such everything has speed, frequency, taste, smell, consistency, sound and colour. This is what we see in the auras. The mentioned characteristics vary according to the data and the knowledge they carry.

These energy masses are either organic, meaning living; or non-organic, meaning not alive. An organic energy is capable of reproduction, like earthlings, vegetation and animals, while non- organic ones don't have the tools to do so. The latter is the processed result of the former. The sole purpose of an organic energy in the Universe is to collect enough knowledge to multiply by division. The impulses in the mind are all organic energies carrying data that has been altered by effects and counter-effects, helping or hindering the owner. If the management is good and the workers do a good job in the centre the results will tilt towards the helping end.

By observing and teaching the interrelation between the unseen soul and the cosmic knowledge, AKIA – the philosophy I have created - gives you the ability to discover and open the depth of the Universe and the mind. The *"everything is interrelated"* slogan offers ample space to the endless, the untouchable and unimaginable quantity of information, and in its explanations an extremely dangerous way of thinking.

In this aspect the beginning, the end and the middle are vague, for every end is a beginning of something and the middle of another happening. We can say the same thing about the other two. I put myself on the plate as an example and since this beginning was chosen by my mind it is not at all illegal to oppose it. However, my choice sets boundaries on the train of my ideas, loosening or tightening their living space. The loosening and the tightening, as the choice of the beginning, depend on the momentary state of my mind, on my relation to the subject and the goal in front of my eyes. The information I have, my knowledge, my scruples, my upbringing, my schooling, my social background, my pledges and my conscience also play a decisive role in my deed. They all alongside many more little ingredients send certain passwords to the brain to test and try the key into the locks of neatly filed folders and into those laying around in lazy untidiness. This action supports the strongest impulse, meaning the most urgent and most important task in the mind waiting to be solved. If I am lucky, one of the keys fits into a lock and I will find few refreshing and helpful thoughts behind the door. Regardless of being conscious - formed under pressure or subconscious - finds its way in without invitation - after creation the thought becomes an organic energy mass. Imagine it like a cartoon where the drawn figures' thoughts are being written on a little, balloon-like surface with an end pointing towards the person that masterminded the thought. This particular earthling would be the starting point of the thought-energy. This is just an example of what is happening in the mind and as such, in the crown chakra. This energy centre is responsible for building channels to receive communication and healing energy from the macrocosm.

Talking about healing I'd like to give you a basic idea of the energy related procedure. As I mentioned earlier, like everything in the Universe, the physical body is made up of segments. They are responsible for the constant motion within. Thought-forms, impulses and effects gather segments of the same polarity to give support to ideas. When another task enters, they move to a different location. It is all well for the constant argument of the 2 poles keep us going. The trouble starts when segments remain in the group permanently. It happens when the human being is unable to release an experience, a thought or a feeling and creates a still - therefore dead - patch within the body which develops into a physical unease, pain and eventually illness. With healing, we reorganize the segments and restart the motion.

BEADBOARD MEDITATION

The meditation - Beadboard[11]

Sit down comfortably with a straight back and your feet on the ground. Inhale slowly counting to 3 and exhale in the same rhythm. Repeat the motion 5 more times.

Imagine a strong beam of golden light descending from above and penetrates your crown chakra on the top of your head. As you inhale it comes down to your base chakra and fills it up. As it is filled by the gift of the Universe project your energy centre out in front of you. It becomes a balloon with events, symbols and words within. Open your diary, the true companion on this journey and write down what you see.

You repeat the exercise with all the big energy centres one by one. When you finished send the golden light back and thank the Universe for its kindness. Relate the seen and heard to your

---

[11] A wooden symbol of wisdom that was placed on the tombs of earthling. The beads represented the numbers of energy centres the person managed to master during his earthly life. The most ancient beadboards were found in Babylon; however, they are still in use by the Hungarian (Magyar) population of Transylvania. The place was annexed to Romania by the treaty of Trianon in 1920.

life and feelings, that are connected to each chakra[12]. Add comments in your diary.

Note

Seeing and hearing will come to you gradually. You should not expect the experience similar to your physical senses but rather a sudden revelation or thought.

Practice

The 12th Century philosopher[13] and Sufi[14], El-Ghazali said: "To the sick man sweet water tastes bitter in the mouth."

Analyse the sentence according to its meaning.

---

[12] Your base chakra is related to your earthly existence: body, material, ties and bonds. A rock there would symbolize a heavy load you carry; people would mean ties, traditions and so on. Although they might be the result of upbringing, social background or religious viewpoint, on the path toward enlightenment an open mind is a must. Your status on the matter becomes apparent by understanding the symbols in the centre.

[13] He is a person who regulates his life by the light of a certain understanding. Philosophy comes from Greek philo that is filing, tidying and Sophia that is pure knowledge.

[14] Sufi is a Muslim mystic who understands the Knowledge in Islam. Here I would recommend the film Bab' Aziz.

EARTH MEDITATION

The meditation - Earth

Sit down on the ground, with your back straightened. Open your knees as much as you can; your arms comfortably beside you or on the knees. Relax.

Breathe slowly and deeply from above through the top of your head. Bring the air down along the spine.

One-two-three-in and one-two-three-out. One-two-three-in and one-two-three-out.

As you are sitting there, imagine that roots are coming out of your sole. Very thin, little roots searching for a channel in the ground. You greet the insects in your way, chat with worms and respectfully lower your head in front of the hard rocks while walking around them. You are searching for water and nourishment. The deeper you get, the thicker you become.

When the roots reach 25 metres under the ground, imagine the black healing energy to shin up from Mother Earth. Do not be afraid of colour black. Remember, everything comes from the earth and the most fertile soil is black. Every inhale brings it further, tickles your sole and caresses your feet. Runs up on the shin and reaches the knees. You see your body losing its original colour gradually and absorbing the black hue of earth, healing your organs and cleansing your digestive system, soothing the ailing points in your body. Cleanse your throat, your tonsils and teeth. Your hair and your nails are all black now and gradually you bland into the energy of the beginning and the end.

You understand that grew out of it and now you want to be part of this magic. Through Mother Earth you become a life giver and a life healer. Your physical body disappears. You are only a small hip of dust that enjoys the warmth of the beaming sun. After a while, the warmth turns into burning. You are thirsty. You need water to survive. You struggle to move grasping for air, weak and almost motionless.

The rain starts up. It is a Godsend. Slowly open your arm and your whole body, your soul to take in more and more from the life-giving force.

As the rain gets heavier and the drops grow, you find it more and more difficult to hold your form and energy together.

You give up the fight. Merge with the water and through the field happily, enjoying the power of the double life-force working in unity.

The rain stops. The Sun comes out again and caresses your scattered body parts. Helps you gather them. First, your head emerges from the ground, your upper body, your arms and finally your legs. Bring your roots back, thank Mother Earth for the healing and the exercise and come back to your earthly existence.

Practice

Take 4 A4 sized sheets of paper.

On the first, write down everything that makes you sad, unhappy, worried, angry or bitter in your life. On the second, note everything that brings you joy, happiness, security or fulfilment. On the third, write down everything you committed against others. On the fourth, you put all you committed against yourself.

Note

These papers should be composed over a month when you dig into your life and discover your inner self.

AKIA-Path-Finder

1. Time is an illusion that imprisons those without courage
2. Life is a constant cycle of personal truth searching
3. Live without bringing shame on yourself
4. You must remake yourself in the eternity of your body
5. The night is not the end of a bad day but the beginning of a better one
6. The outside knowledge is the start of the wisdom within
7. Wisdom is the knowledge you can make use of
8. Material wealth you can inherit, however, true dignity you need to work for
9. Everything you can touch is lent to you for this life. When you leave you cannot take them with you
10. Only through the Universe you can get to know yourself
11. The light embraces you unconditionally and disappears in you if you let it
12. Imagination is the memory of the soul

13. Real knowledge is untouchable and changing

Practice

Please tell us your understanding of each point of the AKIA-Path-Finder.

As the philosophy of the unseen soul and cosmic knowledge, AKIA has guidance to help with understanding earthly living. The Path-Finder is encoded with a cleansing power and mind-opening attributes.

We put tremendous effort into separating religion [15] from spirituality [16].

---

[15] A religion is a set of beliefs and practices centred upon specific supernatural and moral claims about reality and often codified.

[16] Spirituality is a path to reach and become one with the God Force.

AKIA PHILOSOPHY®

APPRENTICE LEVEL

EARTH INITIATION

3

- **Various aspects of earthly living**

Becoming an Earthling is a carefully orchestrated procedure. Souls from all over the Universe plan to enrol in the School of Life. We, earthlings, have this quaint idea, that there is no other existence and souls are queuing up for a place on Earth. It is not so. Souls live and work on every planet using different life forms as protection[17]. However, our planet is different. With the unchangeable uniform, we call the *physical body* it maintains the curiosity of souls willing to learn and speed up the evolutionary path. You will learn much more about the evolutionary path at a later stage of your study.

Nevertheless, there are few important points we need to address: these are *Life tasks*, *Contracts* and *Karma*. Let me start with karma as the most obvious of them.

Although in modern time, we talk about different types of karmas to make the question more complicated and less understandable, it is an intelligent explanation of *what comes around goes around,* meaning that your deeds alter your energy field and as the result, it would attract similar energies. For example, sadness, worry and anger are slow energies and they would attract people with similar feelings.

Reincarnation and karma walk hand in hand. Unresolved situations accumulate strong feelings that make the soul heavy and prevent it to go back to the place it originates from. It is a

---

[17] Hell and Heaven as living spaces for souls before and after earthly existence are only Christian theories. Islam talks about them as a respect towards the People of the Book. However, this story can be easily cracked if you start asking basic questions like where and how. These questions are only valid if you possess some metaphysical knowledge and understand that everything is in constant motion.

simple example of the basic rule of physics. A light object would travel further than a heavy one when they are thrown with the same force. As the result, the soul has no choice but to come back for another life and put a closure on those events. It greatly determines the place and family the soul has to reincarnate into for there is always another soul connected to feelings.

Nearing the Galactic quantum leap on the 28th of December 2012 the Universe redesigned the karmic structure and since February 1972 souls with karma are helped over therefore, reincarnation is not necessary any longer. Since that time only new souls visit the planet without unsolved issues and previous lives here. It is another subject we will talk about to a greater extent later.

Life task is the work plan the soul assign itself to before descending to Earth. The agreement is between the Universe and the soul to further both in evolution.

There are various contracts one also has to live up to. These are signed by individuals or group of souls, who decided to help each other in Earth school. As an example, those who decide to take up learning from us had agreed to it prior to ending up here. Mind you, it is a big part of humanity.

Taking that all on board it is natural that souls within earthly families are not related and they look at life with a totally different approach.

Practice

Observe the members of your family putting emphasis on your parents and children. Look at them as human beings without any social title. I know it feels strange and courage is needed. Write down your observations. I do not want to read sentences like "my mother is the best in the world" or "my father is an honourable man". These views are the fruit of social conventions rather than thinking.

CONTRACTS MEDITATION

The meditation - Contracts

Take the trip to the house on the meadow where you met your guides. Follow the same road but before you get to the house you will notice a creek with a shaky wooden bridge over it. Repair the boards and rails for safe crossing. As you walk take some time to look at your mirror in the water. Walk up to the house. There is nobody there. On the left, there is a door leading into the basement. Follow the steps and as you reach the bottom of the staircase, you'll see a door on your left. Enter the room. The furniture there is scattered and warn; everything is dusty. Next to the door of this room, you'll find a cupboard full of cleaning material, candles, curtains and furniture. Take whatever you need to make your room pretty and homely. Light candles and clean the windows. It is going to be your sacred hideaway. Whenever you want to think about something or want to be by yourself, go down there.

After cleaning and organizing the place, take some biscuits and tea out of the cupboard. Invite your friends to spend some quality time with them. After bidding farewell to your guests, tidy the place again, extinguish the light and candles. Leave the place and walk up the stairs. Your guides are waiting for your smile. Talk to them.

Opposite the entrance door, there is another one that leads to the back yard. Your guides bid farewell and open the door for you. Step out and start walking straight ahead. Very soon you arrive at a path with 17 steps going downwards. While you walk down, think about your connection to people around you and about those you feel particularly close to. Again, forget about family ties for they are social conventions and not soul relations.

At the bottom of the steps, there is a beautiful sandy beach. You notice a big bonfire. Walk up to it and sit down on the sand. As you are gazing into the flames people from all directions would come to you and nod their heads. Some of them are familiar and there are those you have never seen before. You may enter into conversation with them. Please note that these are some of the people you signed a contract with prior to coming down to Earth.

People would leave as they arrive. Finally, you may get up and thank the fire for the help. Walk up the steps, into the house. Walk out the front door and close it behind you. The bridge looks safe this time and your reflection in the water has changed.

Come back and end the same way you have learned in previous meditations.

- **Karma releasing**

All of us were born before the 28th of February 1972 C.E.[18] arrived at Earth with karma. Some of it you might have lived through and some could have been written off from your account.

In February 1992 C.E. new star gateway was opened that allowed the karma to be released into the Universe and dealt with by souls assigned to the task. The event became a necessity to ease the load of the planet and remove the weight of karma.

Karma releasing is a very complex work and I strongly recommend not to attempt it alone, even if the *how* comes from a trusted source.

Here in AKIA, we have collective karma releasing exercise on the first day of the New Moon. Be aware that the above-mentioned calendar doesn't differentiate between the dark moon and the new moon. It is a big mistake where spirituality, healing or ritual system is concerned, for they have distinctive energies and serve different purposes. For karma releasing the New Moon is the only workable energy because the appearance of the silver ball opens the mentioned star

---

[18] Common Era. The calendar we are using has been introduced By Vatican in the 16th century after many attempts to create a system to suit the Church's needs. It is usually referred to as Gregorian calendar. Its belated introduction caused quite a lot of stirs, for dates related to the beginning of the faith and the birth of Jesus was conveniently determined later. It doesn't correspond with nature thoroughly but follows the Sun and its course related to Earth. There are 2 more widely used system: the Jewish calendar that was set up similarly but much earlier than the Gregorian, and the lunar calendar of Islam. The latter follows the cycles of the Moon.

gateway. This day usually follows the one after the new moon according to the calendar. Anyhow, we are going to announce the date and time of the next karma releasing exercise in our newsletter. To take part in this exercise you need to be an apprentice, for basic knowledge and understanding needed to conduct it. However, the most important is the AKIA logo sticker that is despatched to your address at the time you enrol. The logo is a safe communication channel between me and you personally. It is encoded to take care of you during meditations and join the AKIA centre for scheduled healing or communication. Although the sticker might be in a house with many people, it only works for you and not for any of the other members of your family unless they become students.

Now you might have a bitter thought that everything is always about money but I assure you it is not. Money is energy and since in the Universe nothing happens free of charge, it is the easiest way to dispatch the token of your willingness and appreciation.

KARMA RELEASING MEDITATION

Meditation – Karma releasing

The exercise starts with you connecting with the logo. When it is done you open your mind and think about becoming lighter and more able without the burden of karma. Then you start chanting the following mantra[19]:

---

[19] Mantra is a coded, usually repetitive sound to aid your spiritual work.

O-unna-ha-ha, o-unna-ha-ha

You repeat the mantra for as long as you feel it necessary or until you reach the state of the unbearable lightness of being.

- **Connect to the AKIA logo**

Sit down comfortably with a straightened back and your feet on the ground[20]. Imagine a golden beam of light descending from the Universe and penetrates your crown chakra. By a breath of air bring it down into your heart centre. Open it in the front and let the energy connect to the logo in your house.

At the end of the exercise make sure that you disconnect yourself by reversing the connection procedure.

AKIA INVOCATION

GREAT CREATOR,

WHO CREATED THE UNIVERSE, WITH ME IN IT,

TO LOOK AFTER AND FURTHER YOUR MAGNIFICENT WORK,

---

[20] I would like to remind you, that our meditations are astral travellings therefore the Far–Eastern way of meditating cannot be used, for it is to empty the mind more than achieve something with it.

THAT I ACCEPTED IN GOOD FAITH BUT COULD NOT ALWAYS DELIVER

BECAUSE THROUGH MY SELF - CENTEREDNESS

I CHOSE NOT TO SEE ONLY LOOK,

NOT TO LISTEN ONLY HEAR, NOT TO FEEL ONLY THINK.

WITHOUT UNDERSTANDING NATURE'S HARMONIOUS CYCLE,

I STEPPED OUT OF IT, NOT SUSPECTING,

THAT I WOULD NOT BE PROTECTED AND

I WOULD BECOME AN INSTRUMENT OF OUTSIDE FORCES.

PLEASE, GIVE ME THE STRENGTH

TO FORGIVE MYSELF FOR EVERY BAD DEED I COMMITTED

AGAINST ANYBODY AND ANYTHING – INCLUDING MYSELF

WISDOM TO OTHERS TO FORGIVE ME.

SHOW ME THE WAY BACK TO NATURE'S CYCLE

WHERE I CAN LIVE IN PEACE AND DIGNITY,

WITHOUT INDULGING IN SUFFERING,

IN A PLACE,

WHERE LOVE IS UNCONDITIONAL.

Practice:

The mantra that represents the philosophy of the Unseen Soul and Cosmic Knowledge is a complex energy system that heals, opens, attunes, initiates and connects. It is a fast track to us, an emergency number if there is a situation you need help with. Its strength is in the whole, therefore a word by word and a sound by sound learning or chanting is essential. Nothing should be omitted or added to it at any time. Your guides, helpers and communication arrive through it.

Now that you are working on your basic connection to the Universe there is an exercise you need to complete with the mantra.

Print it out and sit down somewhere comfortably. Start reading the mantra. Repeat it 13 x 13 times. Altogether 169 mantras you need to say. You can pose after every 13 but the lot has to be accomplished within the same day you have started.

This exercise creates a distinctive initiation for you, and puts a mark into your energy field. We at AKIA work a lot with the Universe and Earth. Our spirit colleagues bear the same mark to help interrelations.

Think about the meaning behind the words and write your ideas down in the Journal of the Journeys.

- **The fear**

Every slow energy such as anger, sadness, disillusionment, pain and depression in earthly living is created by fear. It is our strongest and only enemy. However, fear is an illusion for we do not really know what it is we are afraid of; actually, that is the cause of the fear.

The Galactic Quantum Leap at the end of the 5th Sun Age[21] on the 28th of December 2012 pushed Earth into the Golden Era[22]. It is all very well but it stopped the predestined way of living and opened avenues for choices and decisions. One of the things earthlings are yearning for is freedom. However, when it presents itself, they do not know what to do with it and it stops looking attractive. Freedom is never physical but mental. The ultimate free spirit is who understands that he is never alone; his belief in the Creator force, we might call nature, and himself is unshakeable. This person understands the spiritual structure of the Universe and the fact that being alone and feeling lonely are very different, for you are always alone but loneliness comes from within.

---

[21] A Sun Age is a time while our Solar System completes a cycle. More about Sun Ages later.
[22] The 5 Sun Ages made up the cycle of the Dark ages after which the whole Galaxy started to ascend towards the Creator force, meaning Light.

The new energy of the Golden Era, The Age of Uranus[23], Global Consumerism and The Protocol[24] push earthlings towards the Knowledge and global understanding. Material security as we have known before disappeared and uncertainty brought in unmeasurable fear instead. This insecurity pushed people into communities either spiritual or religious. Since spirituality is a hard road, religions, especially the powerful Christianity came out as a winner.

FACING YOUR FEARS MEDITATION

Meditation – Facing your fears

Take a trip to your house again. Since you have constructed, the bridge stays from now on. Enter by the front door and greet your guides. If they haven't arrived yet, wait for them. Tell them, that you are on the Path of the 1st Initiation of the Universe, and would like to have their advice blessing for the road ahead.

Bid farewell and leave the house through the backdoor. This door is a star- gateway[25] that now leads to the deepest Sahara. Only golden sand around you, and when you turn to find comfort in the house, just like security, it becomes an illusion and the desert takes its place. There is nobody else, only you

---

[23] Age of Uranus is the result of the Precession of the Equinoxes we will learn about at a later stage.
[24] The plan of achieving the centrally governed New World Order. More about it later.
[25] Star-gate is a space that is cut out of the Universe by a geometrical solid. Star-gateway is a door between two dimensions.

and the mystery-filled Sahara. Start walking led by your intuition[26]. As you walk the Sun gets hotter and your legs heavier. You would like to sit down and rest but you know that that would be the end of your earthly existence. After a while you notice a big black dog walking speedily towards you. It is a real dog, unlike genetically altered pets that depend on mankind for their survival. It is alone and it needs food. The fight is between the two of you and there is only one winner. You can do but fight it and as the triumphant warier you need to taste your enemy by making a feast out of it. Remember, you are fighting your fears now. Like this fierce dog, they lead you off the track and leave you there to perish.

After the feast from the dog, you call the eagles to finish the carcasses.

Continue your walk in the desert until you see a serpent coiling at your feet. Only one bite and your life is over. You need to win this fight. After conquering the serpent prepare a feast from it and let the eagles finish the job.

You are getting more and more tired and wary from the walk and fights. However, you need to stay alert to protect your life from the mystery of the desert. Look under your feet at all times for there are tiny scorpions in the sand preying your last fight in the Sahara would be against one of them. Victory would be followed by a feast that eagles would finish up.

You are tired, the sun is scorching but the journey has to continue until you meet a Sufi sitting in the sand as if he was waiting for you. After greeting him you'll be invited to sit down

---

[26] Intuition is the pure thought coming out of your subconscious. More about it later.

next to him while he talks and tells you moral stories of the desert and Wisdom. Listen carefully and do not forget to preserve them in your journal. Bid farewell and set on your walk home. As a great relief, you'll catch sight of the back door. Step in and greet your guides who are eagerly waiting for you to share your experiences.

Note

These fights represent the everyday struggle we need to go through in order to gain experience and further our evolution. They are not physical fights but mental ones to mirror the physical and mental information you possess about your enemy; your ability to assess situations and speed to act; your will-power; survival instinct and your courage.

Practice

You are alone in the world, without family, friends and colleagues. How would you live your life? What are your plans for the future?

Finding someone to live with or taking on a pet are totally unacceptable propositions!

AKIA PHILOSOPHY®

APPRENTICE LEVEL

EARTH INITIATION

4

- **Prepare for initiation**

AKIA is the philosophy of The Unseen Soul and Cosmic Knowledge therefore the task is to make it accessible for everybody. At this moment we only have the material in English but I am constantly looking for prospective teachers and colleagues with different mother tongue who could translate our teachings.

Initiations usually work centrally when we meet at a given time and I could initiate or you might say attune you with the element of Earth.

On the day of initiation, you cleanse yourself and say the AKIA mantra 13 times. Wear white clothing and build a channel with your logo.

Connect with your teacher online who would say the initiation mantra in front that you need to repeat and add your name when applicable. When finished I would personally attune you.

Note: we organize initiation rituals online twice a year.

MANTRA OF THE 1 INITIATION OF THE UNIVERSE

I ... solemnly promise that the knowledge I gained

I will only use according to the Laws of the Universe.

I clear my thoughts regularly.

I trust the Universe and myself.

Doubts have no place in my life.

Thanks for your trust in me,

That I will always treasure.

Thank you for Blessing me.

Note

Apart from the Old and New Testaments, God by any names always mean the Universe. It is the Higher Force, the Laws of Life, the Quintessence and the First Knowledge that was able to multiply by division. With AKIA you need to open your horizon and go beyond religious views for you are on the path to find yourself and not a religion.

This path is rockier but much more rewarding. You'll gain a vast amount of information and arrive at understand more and more interrelations of events. You'll lose your fear and develop great respect for Life. And one day you'll realize that you need to bear responsibility for your deeds, words and thoughts because you are a co-creator.

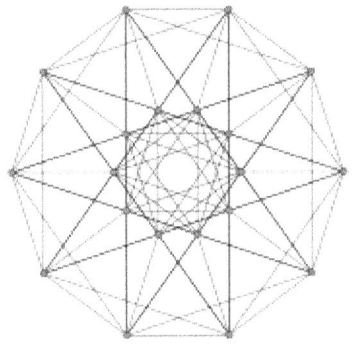

AKIA PHILOSOPHY®

APPRENTICE LEVEL

RELEASE THE SPRING OF LIGHT WITHIN

1

We are fortunate enough to have quite a lot of choices concerning our spiritual growth. Courses and workshops are offering possibilities to find the path and the meaning of life with it. Some of them are excellent. However, many of them fail to offer the basic understanding of existence. Without foundation, the information is floating around and makes living more confusing than ever.

To comprehend the concept of earthly living is not that hard. Just like a fairy tale we imagine the story and sometimes even accept certain part of it as real.

Acceptance is good but the wisdom comes from experience when one releases the information into practice. And it is hard. We like to cling to things and thought forms regardless of their quality.

During the 2160 years of the Pisces and Neptune era religions and capitalism put so much fear into our head that we forgot not just to use our abilities, but also about their existence. Intuition was labelled with words like fantasy, dream, illusion, and truth was reduced to the mere physical state.

In this workshop I teach you how to **cleanse the soul** from the **withholding essence of previous lives, karmas, thought forms, family ties and connections**.

We go through the **4 basic elements** as the foundation of the physical body, the cause of **incarnations and reincarnations**, the **Duty** and the **Contract**. Also touch upon **Atlantis** as the beginning of earthly living, the **Universal School** for the ever-developing souls. You learn the energy system of an earthling like yourself, to see, feel and hear beyond the boundaries of the physical body.

In one word we put you on the path to the four-dimensional existence, the foundation for the energies of the Golden Era that started on the 28th of December 2012 c.e. The 5th Sun Age[27] ended then as the Galaxy leaped into a higher dimension.

- **The light we are searching for**

The light we are after is the Gnosis, the Haya Sophia, the Opus Magnum, the Beginning and the End, the Great Knowledge of Humanity and the Universe. As one starts the walk on the path of enlightenment, the light of Wisdom takes over from the darkness of Ignorance and the earthling emerges from the Jahiliyyah[28].

Somewhere in the physical body there is a dormant sparkle in every earthling[29]. Very much alike planet Earth herself. As a human physical body is an exquisite alchemical blend of the planet, it behaves similarly. However, while the sparkle within the centre of Earth is pretty much alive, so is its connection with the Universe, earthlings need to work on finding and awakening the fire within.

---

[27] A Sun Age is a period of time while the Solar System completes a circle around the centre of the Galaxy. We are going to learn more about them at a later date.
[28] Jahiliyyah is an Arabic word used to describe the dark state of existence prior to finding the path towards the light of knowledge.
[29] I call earthling every human being with a soul.

This is the point we refer to as Hara[30]. Although it is said to be the place of balance, I would translate it as the meeting point of the Micro and Macro cosms within the essence of every earthling. Sometimes I call it the Centre of Gravity that keeps us connected to the Hara of the planet and as spiritual evolution takes us further, it will be the place that connects us to the Universe. It has been said that Hara is a chakra. No, but in the awaken state it is always in one of the major energy centres.

In the dormant state the Hara is under the Base chakra. It is the place where the Djed column starts in Egyptian Knowledge, Kundalini sleeps according to Eastern understanding, and Malkuth is in Jewish mysticism.

At the awakening time, Hara slips into the lowest energy centre, the Base chakra where it starts the journey towards the light.

The most ancient symbol of this journey is the Rod of Hermes[31], the Caduceus[32]. Later on, your path towards the Light, they will be mentioned again.

---

[30] Hara is one of those Sanskrit words that lost its real meaning after the introduction of religions.
[31] Hermes is the Greek name of Imhotep, the Egyptian educator, healer and architect.
[32] Caduceus is also a Greek name of the winged-sun-topped staff with the two coiling snakes. Unfortunately, during the last 250 years the symbol has been adopted by modern medicine, the US army and many other organizations, which have nothing to do with Knowledge, and diluted its meaning on the way.

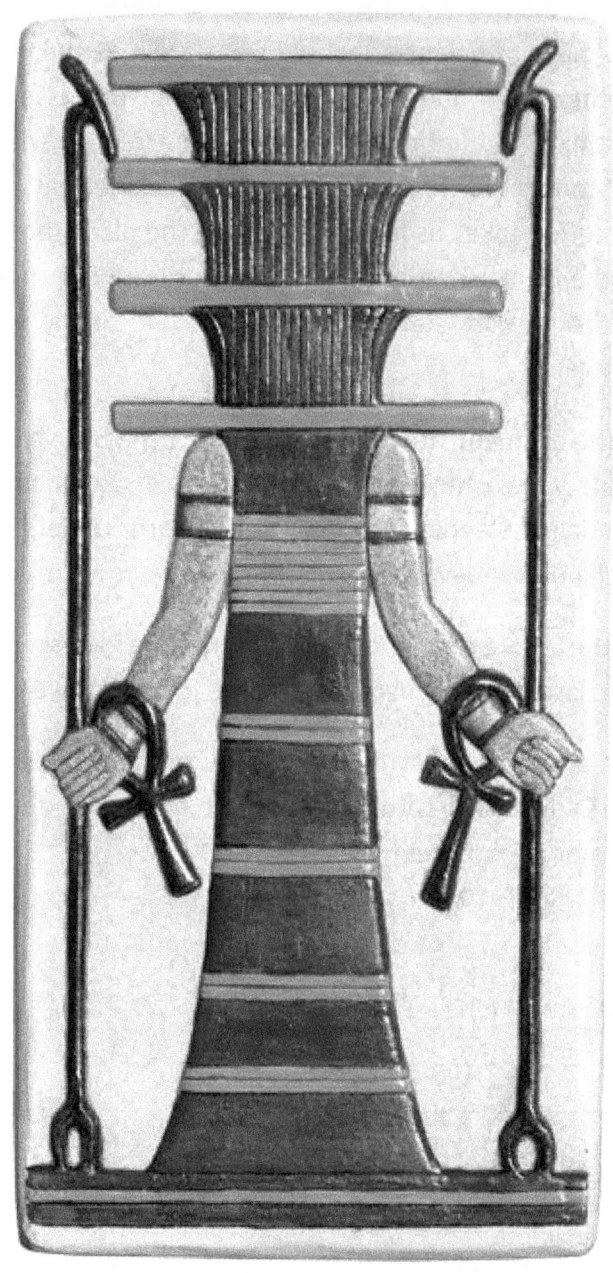

- **The path of the Light**

As you know an earthling has 3 bodies: physical, spiritual and astral. The physical body is closely connected to Earth, the astral body is to the Universe and the spiritual is in communication with both. The 3 bodies represent the 3 microcosmic elements: earth, water and air. As the elements, the bodies are also connected with a fine thread. Prior to embracing the light, these connections are not conscious. It is a state of existing in separation. During the Pisces Era[33], that started around 200 b.c.e[34], the remaining Knowledge was broken into segments and started the deliberate journey into the abyss of the past. This is still the favourite method for destructive forces on Earth. Great powers cut up countries and companies in the process of wiping them clean. Since it is a slow and very painful death, there is no energy for uprising or protest; mere survival gobbles up all the strength of those affected.

Everything in the Universe is interrelated. It is an organic matrix. Either you like it or not, the nearer to the centre you are the more involved you become. The aggressor might have more material in life but he is strapped off of his dignity and becomes the struggler where conscious existence is concerned. In this sense there are no losers or winners in life. As the result the above-mentioned approach, today many earthlings refer to

---

[33] Due to the Precession every 2,160 odd years the Sun rises in the court of another star formation during the Spring Equinox. These planetary events are called the Precession of the Equinox. We will talk about them later.
[34] Before Common Era

love life, carrier and private life as separate aspects of living, without understanding the alchemical blend of energies.

At the early time of awakening the earthling gets conscious of the physical body and let his life be governed by material, earth bounded physical products and this body is the centre of attention. Eyes are used as ruling senses.

As the Light gets brighter the spiritual body gradually gains strength and its connection with the physical body strengthens. The interrelation of thoughts and emotions become clearer and the governing role is taken by the spiritual body as they embrace. Senses such as smelling and touching sharpen.

As Light from the Hara is moving towards the Universe the astral body starts bringing in the fire element and the Knowledge with it. Development speeds up, boundaries expand and gradually disappear; The 3 bodies merge and existence will be governed by the astral body. The earthling becomes wholesome, the perfect alchemical blend of the Universe. His life is powered by the Great Knowledge as he is connected to the Creator Force, the Light, and walks the path to become the Light himself.

During the journey the Hara travels up on the spine and takes up residence in the appropriate chakra until it reaches the highest level, the Crown that is the Winged Sun, Kether, the Sahasrara centre with the thousand petals, representing the only reality possible, the Royal Embrace.

Practice

I invite you to look at your life and assess it according to the information given to you. The questions to pursue are:

- Where do I come from? – social background and understanding of living, favourite colours, music, films, books, leisure time activities, views of life
- Where am I? – I mean emotionally, professionally and mental understanding of all the above questions.
- What are my aims?

- **The meeting of the 2 triangles from the Micro and Macro cosms.**

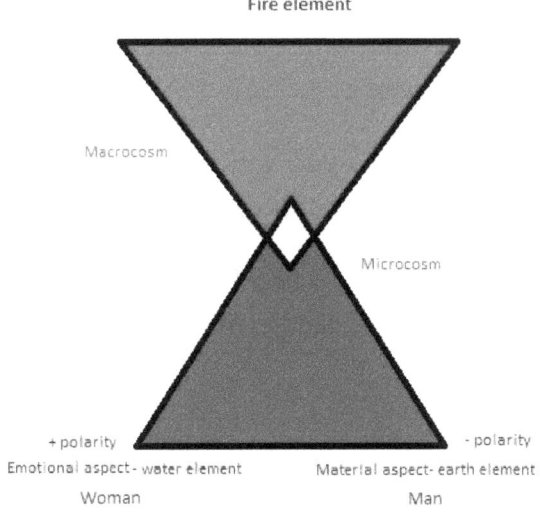

DJED CLEANSING MEDITATION

The meditation – lighting the candle within – Djed cleansing

Sit down comfortably with straight back and your feet on the ground. Inhale slowly counting to 3 and exhale in the same rhythm. Repeat the motion 5 more times.

Imagine a strong beam of golden light descending from above and penetrates your crown chakra on the top of your head. As you inhale it comes down to your base chakra and fills it up. As it is filled by the gift of the Universe project your energy centre out in front of you. It becomes a balloon with events, symbols and words within. Open your diary, the true companion on this journey and write down what you see.

You repeat the exercise with all the big energy centres one by one.

When you finished send the golden light back and thank the Universe for its kindness.

Relate the seen and heard to your life and feelings connected to each chakra. Add comments in your diary.

After you are thoroughly cleansed from blockages and residues you are ready to light the candle, meaning the dormant sparkle, in your Hara.

Imagine the same golden light coming through your crown chakra as before. Bring it down into the heart chakra. Let it warm you and give you a feeling of trust, present and future. Then send it down into the Solar Plexus, where rituals, such as this, take place. Project your chakra out as you have already learnt and with the strength of your mind, furnish it with a round table. It is a simple table with 4 legs, natural, wooden unfinished piece. There is a white, unlit candle in the middle,

Now look above your head. Imagine that there is a ball of bright, silvery-golden light hovering there, waiting for invitation. Let this ball into your body and feel as it travels through the upper chakras and stops in the Solar Plexus. You see as the light approaches the candle on the table; lit it and speedily disappears, back to the universe, following the route it came in.

You feel warm and content. Gaze into the candlelight, without focusing on it, and listen to your intuition.

Bring in your chakra with the lit candle and thank the universe for the help.

Note

This candlelight is the channel between you and the universe. All information and Knowledge coming to you through this route is filtered by your own understanding of the world. The wider your horizon is the more you may learn.

Please do appreciate, that you need to follow my directions to the dot to stay within the safety zone. It is my priority to keep you earth bounded to the extent necessary in order to achieve that. The AKIA logo, which you should have by now, is a good help in our work. The incoming Knowledge has to be regulated according to individual intelligence and eagerness to succeed. Boundaries need to be pushed beyond the comfort zone just enough to allow the Light in. As new information settle, they gradually become part of the extended comfort zone.

- **Light[35] cleansing and healing**

The source of light for Earth and its inhabitants is the big fireball. As the centre and pulling power of the Solar system He is the master energy manipulator and caretaker.

As a student of AKIA, you enjoy many privileges that you will understand while travelling in time and space. One of those valuable perks is to be allowed to visit the Sun. Although the Sun is practically not a planet, due to some kind of classification, as an energy mass it behaves as one.

VISIT THE SUN MEDITATION

The meditation – Visit the Sun

I have mentioned earlier that imagination, fantasy and illusion are not falser than the so-called *tangible* objects or subjects we label *truth*. They are both the work of the mind and closely related to the creative power of the individual.

---

[35] Light is the symbol of knowledge. Knowledge is information which has been built into the energy field by experience. It is something you understand and not believe. Questions, like *why* and *how,* should be asked constantly to enable new information turning into knowledge. Do not be afraid of getting rid of information in case it doesn't fit. One day, when your perception arrives there, you might say: *Yes, now I understand!* Or you dismiss it from your system forever.

I create every meditation to serve the sole purpose horizon stretching. Naturally I am responsible for keeping you safe, therefore it sets the boundaries to stretching boundaries.

Sit down comfortably with straight back and your feet on the ground. Inhale slowly counting to 3 and exhale in the same rhythm. Repeat the motion 5 more times.

Imagine a golden stream of energy from above coming through your crown chakra. Do not forget, ***it has to be golden***. Your breathing is the carrying vehicle of the most precious healing and cleansing substance. As you inhale the golden energy gradually fills you, and your astral body will be connected to a higher plane of existence. This connection is temporary, for similar energies like each other, and without this higher plane in your everyday life you can only be exposed to this energy for a short period of time. The supervision needed comes from us through your personal AKIA logo.

Let the light fill your body, let it flow into your aura and expand it to 3 metres in diameter. You are a miniature sun now with the same power, the light and knowledge.

Hold one of your hands out, palm up. Imagine that there is a scale vertical scale in front of you with the 7 major chakras on it. You find that your Hara is moved up into one of these chakras. Put your palm under it and slowly push it up into the crown chakra. You feel the weight against your palm. When your centre of gravity arrived into the highest centre, you feel that your whole existence lifts up from the ground and you feel a floating sensation. Push your palm further until you arrive into the Sun as a response to its pulling power. Let yourself be caressed by the warmth and light. Listen to your intuition and observe the surrounding. When you start feeling tired, put your palm out again, looking downward this time and push your Hara down slowly until you arrive back to your previous existence.

Thank the Universe and the Sun for the experience.

Write down your experience.

Note

It is a great daily exercise for healing your immune system.

AKIA PHILOSOPHY®

APPRENTICE LEVEL

RELEASE THE SPRING OF LIGHT WITHIN

2

- **Cycles in the microcosm**

Life is a chain of events. As we look at those events, they all have a beginning and an end. These 2 points are determined by the related persons' individual understanding of the particular event. Naturally every end is the beginning of another cycle and there are many ends and beginnings between ends and beginnings. Although everything is interrelated hence infinite, nevertheless the 2 points are always needed, to draw the road that leads to the goal. As the result of consumerism and worshipping of the Materia, earthlings have this impatience to rush everything in the misconception of a better life at the end.

A perfect cycle is a circle: always has the aim in sight, covers every detail necessary and consciously learning on the road. However, in practice perfect cycles do not exist. Human beings with a full life cannot afford to focus on one aim only. There are also lesser goals on the sides in need for imminent attention. Only real conscious determination could keep one alert and push one forward, towards the original aim. Nevertheless, side roads bring valuable information and experience which eventually turn into support. The deeper one gets into learning, the bigger the danger is that the lesser aims on the side roads grow out of proportion and take over. There are also times when it becomes clear that the original main aim was a lure towards the hidden but more valuable path. On the other hand, many earthlings are on the surface. Without relating to responsibilities, they travel through everything and everybody to arrive at the aim they set up. The cycles of those resemble a straight line more than a circle.

The size of a particular cycle is determined by the closure or the end of the path as a result of decision making or a helping hand from the Universe. By finishing the path, the circle of the train thoughts and aims is closed. Since we cannot go back where we have been before, for it doesn't exist any longer, life continues on a higher level due to the lessons learnt. This is what we call the quantum leap and with it the circle turns into a spiral.

Some earthlings have the illusion of being in control. Others shift the responsibility on the shoulder of a deity and give into *"che sera, sera"*, the syndrome of take what comes. However, there are strong planetary cycles affecting us on everyday basis; playing with our nerves, pushing us towards experiences and altering our viewpoints concerning the life on Earth. These are permanent and unchangeable cycles. Whatever humanity does to change the course of nature, the cycles of the Sun, Moon, the ruling planets[36], the Precessions of the Equinoxes[37] and planetary alignments will stay to guide, rule and alter.

---

[36] Due to the build-up of slow energies Earth became heavier that resulted in a shorter course around the Sun. About 70 – 80 years ago the 12-star formations zodiac, which was on the ecliptic, got out of alignment. However, the ruling planets are still at work. As an example, Aquarius has no meaning for us any longer but Uranus is there, pushing us towards awakening and knowledge.

[37] In this context we only talk about the Spring Equinox that happens at the Full Moon around the end of March or beginning of April. Since Earth cannot complete a whole cycle around the Sun in the course of a calendar year, during approximately 2160 years the ruling planet of this day slips back.

Note

More about Moon cycles and Sun Ages please refer to page 3 in Earth Initiation 1.

We'll talk more about planetary movements at a later stage.

STRENGTHEN YOUR IMMUNE SYSTEM MEDITATION

The meditation – Strengthen your immune system in the Sun

Do the preliminary steps required before every mediation: sit down comfortably, your back straightened and your feet on the ground. Set the slow rhythm of your breathing: one - two – three in and one – two – three out.

Imagine that roots are growing from your feet and get firmly into the ground. As you inhale you bring in the black healing energy of mother Earth while with exhaling it is distributed to every segment of your body, collecting residues and healing your organs. When your whole body is cleansed, you invite the golden light through the crown chakra. It is important that you imagine the brightest of lights coming from above. As you inhale the light fills your body washing the black earth energy with the residues and illnesses. Do not stop inhaling the golden knowledge from the universe. Let it flow into your aura, expand it, until you become a huge golden balloon,

Enjoy the airy feeling bouncing back and forth. Let yourself leave the boundaries of the planet and slowly aim for the Sun. On arrival you'll find yourself in a big and lushes garden with the most exquisitely coloured flowers. As you get accustomed to the light and energy you are able to see more and more of the Southern star-gate. There are buildings and different types of creatures are doing their work.

If you turn left from the place of entry, you'll find a building there. Knock on the door and without further ado, enter the building. It houses the immune system strengthening machinery that has been especially designed for earthlings. There are souls and entities [38] getting on with their work assigned to them. You do not need to communicate. Look around while you are waiting your turn.

You will be taken to cleanse and boost your body to withstand the harsh changes in food, air and water on Earth. I do not describe the event because I want you to observe and take notes of it.

When finished, you find the exit and let yourself gently fall back to Earth.

Note

This meditation is good for everyday usage to heal and strengthen your immune system.

---

[38] Entities are organic energies trained and assigned to do certain works in the Universe. Entities are not immortal; they do not multiply and they are only capable of doing the task they are trained for initially.

Practice

Cycles in your life – exercise

Observe the cycles in your life. Do they have aims? What is the concept behind your aims? Are you strong enough to follow the aim? What do you learn on the road? Do you like shorter or longer aims more? Why?

- **2012 as the end of the Great Cycle**

As you know life is a chain of cycles with ends and beginnings, all of which are greatly influenced by the planetary movements around us. Every motion has ups and downs. Like a rollercoaster after up comes down and vice versa. The higher the up is the deeper the down gets.

The first 5 Sun Ages represented the darker and deeper side of human existence. It was designed to prepare earthlings for the Reign of the Golden Light after the Galactic Quantum Leap on the 28th of December 2012 c.e.

During the 22 250 years of the Five Sun Ages, Earthlings have been taken through the 4 element initiations one by one at the end of each Sun Age to enable earthlings to embrace the Light and Knowledge.

The end of the 1st Sun Age, in b.c.e 16 230, the Haudi[39] Solar System received the 1st initiation and became aligned with Earth element. The Maya looks at it as the Era of Water probably because the understanding of attachments to the

---

[39] The cosmic name of the solar system where Earth is.

planet and to other organic energies initiated the separation movement that was actually fulfilled in the 2nd Sun Age.

Apart from the obvious magnetic connection to the planet, Earth as an element is responsible for attachments, ties, Earthly belief systems like religions, behaviour patterns, genetic inheritance, social background and everything material. Looking at globalisation, the consumerism and the growing importance of the materia, it is vital to understand and harmonize Earth element within. This is the first, the most important and the most difficult initiations of the four.

The traumatic energy changes at this Solar Quantum Leap resulted in major movements of the ground. As a result, Atlantis, the cradle of Earthlings broke to several pieces and shifted into the ocean.

The end of the 2nd Sun Age in b.c.e.12 220, the Haudi solar system received its 2nd initiation and became aligned with the element of Water. The Maya calls it the era of The Wind-Serpent. The name announces the arrival of the 3rd element and that is Air.

4 081 years later, in b.c.e. 8 139 arrived the end of the 3rd Sun Age. According to Maya, Fire finished it and gave ways to the 4th Sun Age when Fire was the main element.

As we mentioned before, Fire comes from the Universe. It is a symbol of Pure Knowledge that is only available in the Macrocosm. It was the time for earthlings to learn the power of the Self and the Meaning of Life.

The 4th Sun Age has also ended in fire in 3 113 b.c.e. It is the time when humanity had the opportunity to get into alignment with the Creator Force or Universe, we might call it. It is the time when Venus arrived into Haudi as the ambassador of peace and the ever-burning torch for lost souls. It is the time when Maya created the famous calendar that took us to the end of the 5th Sun Age on the 28th of December 2012 c.e. According to their prediction life and the planet should have ended there. However, we made it through the leap and earned a chance to change.

Note

This cycle exists in everything we do, feel or think.

IN THE CANDLE MEDITATION

The Meditation – In the candle

Warning! In this meditation you step out into space with your astral body. It is important that you connect to logo before you start.

Connecting to the logo – please refer to Earth Initiation 3

Start your meditation as the Beadboard exercise. However, instead of working with your whole chakra, when you project it out one by one, divide them each into 7 levels. It represents the seven steps of existence within each energy centres; like chakras within a chakra. As always start with the base and the lowest segment. Observe the colour of the segment, take note of it and with the golden light from the Universe cleanse it until it becomes gold. Continue with the next segment. When you finish with a chakra, take on the next one until you cleansed all seven. Please take notes of the colours you see for they show your momentary relation to your world, life and the Universe. When you finished, project the golden light from your heart energy centre and start walking. You are out there, all the planets around you. Take notes. As you walk you see a big candle, taller than you, on the roadside that might be burning. If not, you need to light it.

Walk around the candle, touching its side to find the way in. When it opens walk into it. There are few chairs and other different types of furniture. Sit down and inhale the energy of knowledge and healing. You might want to use this opportunity to look at confusing situations or ideas in your life. Use your notebook.

When you finished, ask your guides to come. Talk with them.

After the conversation, say bye-bye and step out of the burning candle. Extinguish the light, say thank you to the Universe and walk home the way you came. Pull back the golden light from your heart chakra, release it to the Universe. Say thanks and come back to your everyday existence.

Note

This is a meditation that you can do daily if you wish so. For communication with your guide or finding clear understanding of situations it is an excellent practice.

- **The role of Earthlings - the essence of existence**

Looking at Earth as the essential part of the whole we come to realize that we are all important and as such have certain duties and responsibilities towards the Self and others.

It is very naive to think that what is far away it doesn't affect you and it is not part of your responsibility. Either you like it or not everything comes back to you; and since you are our student you belong to the very small group who really wants to understand and see the hidden meanings behind closed doors. I say it again, it is very possible that one day you wake up and curse the day you lost your *innocence* to AKIA, but you need to understand that it had to happen. We, you and I, signed a contract about working together and help each other to climb the ladder towards the Light. Obviously, you can still choose to ignore the call, but do not get frightened of obstacles. Turn to us, tell us your doubts and if there is a way to help, we would definitely do it.

The answer to the question about the essence of existence is a turning point. The initial shift is in the question itself. It means that a thought was formed towards gaining understanding of life.

The essence of existence on Earth is simple. The planet is a school where earthlings need to build a bridge between the conscious and the subconscious to let the knowledge out and implement it into earthly living. The conscious contains information has been collected during this life on this planet, while the subconscious has all that the soul learnt throughout its lifetime.

As in every school, keywords are given to the students to find the knowledge related to the subject and bring it to light. That is why we say that here on Earth, one doesn't learn anything new, but one is reminded the knowledge one already has. The difference is in the filters, the 2 earthly element Earth and Water. The first represents the Materia and the second is Emotion. As water and earth are connected, they cannot exist without each other. In earthly living the Materia is given by the physical body and emotions are tied to the wellbeing of it. Emotions are the result of thoughts about material related to your life. Here I remind you that your body, its needs, desires and demands are all material. Therefore, the essence of existence is to understand these 2 elements and rise above them to follow the path towards the Source. However, it cannot be done by skipping them as religions are suggesting. The full understanding of the 2 elements is required to the evolution of the soul.

Practice

Look into your life and find out what is the material drive behind your deeds, wishes and desires. Be honest with yourself and do not forget, that to a certain extent, we need the materia!

FACE YOUR EMOTIONS MEDITATION

The meditation – Face your emotions

Start, as you always do, with the preliminary breathing and cleansing exercise. The latter could be any of your choice.

Connect to the logo.

Draw the road with the golden energy of the Universe and start walking. Observe everything on the way.

You walk until you see a beautiful lake on your right. The water is surrounded by rear species of the vegetation kingdom. You may touch them, event talk to them if you wish. They all carry knowledge from faraway galaxies.

As you done with the conversation, step on the water. Do not be afraid even if you are not a good swimmer. It is an astral projection; we might call hologram that works with the logo well together. Believe in yourself, and understand that you are not alone for the Universe would always help you on the path towards fulfilment.

As you walk the water opens up in front of you and through a channel you find yourself in the kingdom under the water. The palace is in front of you and you are escorted to the King by the name of Arishan.

Introduce yourself and tell him that you are working on a quest. Ask him if you have any thoughts, he is willing to share with you.

After the conversation bid farewell, and following your intuition, find a room where you feel at home. Clear your thoughts and emotions.

Find your way back, merge from the water, walk to the shore and follow the yellow brick road back to earthly existence. Send back the golden energy and thank the Universe for the help.

Take notes on the journey

AKIA PHILOSOPHY®

APPRENTICE LEVEL

RELEASE THE SPRING OF LIGHT WITHIN

3

- **Contracts and tasks**

With the Golden Era[40] a new kind of life beckoned. Fast, high frequency energy comes from the reigning Uranus and pre-written Life Path is reduced to Contracts and Tasks. Everything happens in order to save the planet and humanity with it. Earth is an old planet that needs uplifting and rejuvenation to get back on its original course within the solar system.

The weight of responsibility is on the shoulder of humanity. Earthlings need to understand this responsibility and bear it. Decisions have to be made daily. Undecided situations halt the machinery of happening and the energy exchange. It scatters the seeds of doubt in the immediate vicinity that spreads the insecurity further. Until someone with strength and conviction steps up and stops the epidemic.

Furthermore, if you do not make the decision, somebody else will step in and make it for you; because without decision the world stops.

Governments, world organizations work similarly. We get angry with politicians when they make decisions we do not like. However, we give them the power and let them do what they want. Therefore, the responsibility falls back on us.

Contracts are usually connected the evolution of the soul. It could be a romantic relationship, friendship, workmanship or just an acquaintance passing through. Whichever it is teaching and learning are involved. When contracts are sealed, they cannot be broken. In some cases, a party or parties are allowed to get out of them in exchange for some hardship as a learning

---

[40] Time after the cycle of the 5 Sun Ages and the Galactic Quantum Leap.

substitute, and there are rare occasions when there is no punishment attached to a broken contract.

Task is the special duty you sign up for prior to descend. It always goes further and directly adds to the Universe. Naturally working with the Universe comes with personal evolution but in these cases the pure aim is to further the Macrocosm.

Contracts and tasks are *written* and possible to look at with a guided tour. We will learn more about the subject at a later stage.

BEADBORD MEDITATION

The meditation – Beadboard

Please refer to earlier lessons.

Notes should be taken during or after the meditation

Practice

What kind of changes would you like to implement on Earth to make it a better place? What is a good living environment for you? How can you personally improve your environment?

Note

Few things you need to bear in mind with this exercise: prior to descend you have chosen the place and the family where you are. Also, there is no point saying phrases like *I dream about world peace* or *good health and wealth*. These words are illusions, and dreaming is idle, unless you make an effort and put your thoughts into practice.

- **The soul - its origin and earthly life**

In order to understand the subject, one needs to arrive at the conclusion that souls live all over in the Universe. However physical body is only needed on Earth and on the other 15 earth-like planets. Star gateways are also places where dense body forms might be used. You'll find that certain subjects pop back into the education cycle in AKIA. At the beginning passwords are given to you with basic information. As your horizon is widening, you are able to take in more about subjects already familiar to you.

Let us get back to the soul. As we have already established everything is energy in the Universe. As such everything possesses all the characteristics of the energy in the physical sense. These are colour, smell, substance, taste, sound and speed, frequency, polarity. Apart from polarity the rest of the data makes up the real essence of the soul. These are the past lives, the learnt and unsolved lessons, emotional experiences, way of thinking and evolutionary state, and also the momentary thoughts and the physical status of the bearer. In the case of earthlings, the physical body becomes the part of the soul and works as a mirror and reminder. Together they make up the unique knowledge that identifies the soul. These are the vibes psychics pick up on and others relate to. Here I would like to mention that every soul living on Earth as an earthling has psychic power. The degree depends on the spiritual development of the soul.

The earthly life of the soul starts long before descending. Either the soul chooses to spend some time on Earth or is sent down to accomplish a particular task, there are several arrangements to be made. Similarly, to conscious development on Earth an aim is needed to draw the road. All aims are connected to emotions and emotions exist due to the physical body. Think about it! What would life be without the physical body? Everything we do and call living is connected to it!

Without psychical body the soul cannot survive on Earth. There is a strong magnetic pull from the planet that imprisons everything within. Due to this dense aura, the pure energy of the Universe, what souls feed on, is not accessible from Earth. Therefore, a link is needed, through which the Prana, the Life Force could reach us. This link is the physical body that extracts the nourishment from other organic energies like vegetation and animals. The digestive system is the most complex chemical plant known to earthlings. There is also a need for producing little physical bodies for new souls wishing to come down here.

The physical body is the key to the lessons in Earth School. Everything we do, think or say is related to it one way or another. It is the tool we use for experiencing and learning. It is the channel between the Macro and the Micro Cosms as well as between the conscious[41] and the subconscious[42]. During earthly living the soul needs to learn to use the physical body as a bridge between the 2 planes, discover the extraordinary deeds it is capable of and understand that Prophet mythologies (Buddha, Moses, Jesus) are true, not because they are the sons of God or in any way chosen, but because they symbolize the true potentials of a human being. After all we are all children of God so to speak; or as I would say we come from the same source with very similar subconscious knowledge.

It is very interesting to observe how very little we know our physical body. I am not talking about the erotic zones – we do not really understand them either – but simple tasks like walking, carrying things, posture, use muscles, chew and eat and so on. And since general education mainly focuses on consumerism, many people end up with a bone problem, posture disorder and distorted body. Also, important to know that even the best exercise only works well with perfect bones and muscles.

The way you walk, the way you hold yourself is the mirror of your behaviour pattern and comprehension of the whole.

---

[41] Conscious is the storage for all the events, lessons, experiences and wisdom the soul acquired during this lifetime. Please note that lesson and wisdom are states of mind that you are aware of.

[42] Subconscious is the storage for everything the soul went through prior to this life.

Practice

How your everyday deeds and thoughts relate to your physical body? Give 20 examples. Is there anything in life you cannot connect with it?

Note

This exercise might seem easy however finding relations between feelings and thoughts need deep thinking and understanding. Everything has a cause behind the scene and the cause has yet another cause and so on.

Practice

Examine your body and your habits related to it, such as stamping, fidgeting, leaning, gestures and so on. What do they mean? What emotion are they related to?

- **Energy interrelations**

As a reminder I mention that everything in the Universe is energy. Either organic or non – organic. Organic energies are able to reproduce while non – organic cannot. When I say reproduce, I think of healing and tissue reproduction as happens with living creatures. The data – such as speed, frequency, fragrance, taste, substance, colour and sound – of an energy are interrelated and mirror the behaviour pattern of the energy. Together they show the Knowledge and the evolutionary level of the object or subject in question. As an example, a denser substance would have darker colour and lower sound, while higher frequency would produce lighter colours and higher sounds.

Apart from the above mentioned features every energy mass has polarity. It is either positive or negative depending on the segment structure of the unit. Please bear in mind that positive and negative polarity energy doesn't in any way equal to the colloquial terms used very often today. Positive energy is not better or worse than negative. I never fully understand what people mean by these phrases. They cannot be substitutions for good or bad for a positive result at any kind of medical office confirms that something is not right and they might be accompanied with pain and suffering. On the other hand, there is no good or bad in total clarity anywhere, for where is good there is bad. The 2 poles are in everything. Good or bad people do not exist. The equal amount of opposite resides in everything. Due to the spiritual development of the certain energy, one of the poles would become stronger. It is also important to understand that good or bad are individual viewpoints: what is good for you might be very bad for you and what seems good today might turn out to be disastrous tomorrow.

Everything happens for a reason and everybody always gives 100% of his/her abilities at every given moment. Reasoning, such as *I could have done better* has no place in life. It is the result of the brain, not the mind.

- **More about your fears**

Although we come up with the most colourful explanation for our misfortune or mishaps in life, they are due to only one thing and it is fear. The problem starts with education when we come across words like misfortune and mishaps. Both means that powers out of reach, control and understanding are playing tricks on us and we have no ways to foresee or deal with them. I do not want to sound bold to suggest that you are able to control everything. Far from it! I only say that the more you know the more you are able to see the influences beyond your control. However, control comes from understanding and the source of this is knowledge.

In the Universe there is nothing that cannot be understood or relate to Earthly existence. *As above so below* goes the saying that made Hermes Trismegistos[43] so famous and immortal.

Let us stop here for a moment and think about the sentence. What is the above and the below? What does it mean? Do you have any example in mind?

Getting back to fear, it is the greatest enemy of humanity. It is an enemy very difficult to fight, for it is within us. We nurture it and it feeds on us. The longer it is nurtured the more it eats and the weaker you become. Until one day it takes over and uses you for food.

---

[43] Hermes Trismegistos is the Greek name given to Imhotep, the architect, healer and accountant of the Sun God, the pharaoh of Khem, the place, we call Egypt today. Hermes depicts the messenger with the winged feet whose ability to travel between planes and dimensions are beyond common imagination. Tri means 3 x and Megistos carries the meaning of the ultimate greatness.

As with everything, it is easy to deal with fear if you understand it and know how. Fear, as all the other feelings, derives from the mind. It is a result of not knowing or not understanding something. If you think about it, we are afraid because we do not know what will happen. We are afraid of the unknown. If it is unknown, what are we afraid of exactly?

Fear is an illusion that poisons life. It gets into the mind unnoticed and spreads there taking over more and more space, until it is stopped and turned around. Or consumes your life.

Practice

Grab some paper and pen. Start writing down what are you afraid of? Why do you fear those events? Is there a thought form behind it? Upbringing? Tradition? Education?

When you finished, please think about solutions to eliminate your fear.

Observe people around you. What are their fears? How do they tackle them?

FEAR RELEASING MEDITATION

The meditation – releasing your fear

Sit down comfortably with straight back, your feet on the ground. Harmonize your breathing by inhaling for the count of 3 and exhaling for the count of 3. Keep going for about a minute. Then, while you continue with the rhythm of your breathing, open your crown chakra and let the golden energy of the Universe into your body. Release it through the heart chakra to draw the path. Follow the golden thread of energy observing the walk and take note of all the experiences.

You arrive at a large lake. Step on the water very carefully and start walking on it gracefully with your back straight and your head up. Gaze on the endless water in the distance and listen to what it says. Without warning at a step, the water sucks you in and you go through a channel to find yourself in an underwater palace.

As you look around there is a wardrobe on your left. Open it up and take an outfit to change into. As you walk from room to room, spend some time in every one of them and listen to your thoughts. Enter into conversation with anybody around.

At the end you arrive at big hall, full of interestingly dressed, human-like souls. There is a celebration going on. Take part in it, mingle and enjoy.

When you decide to leave, go back to the end of the building. Change your clothing and step into the water as it opens up to allow you to surface. Walk back to the shore. Find the golden path that leads you to your earthly existence. Pull back the golden thread and release it through the Crown chakra. Thank the Universe for the help and experience.

Note:

All your experiences should be noted in your journal.

AKIA PHILOSOPHY®

APPRENTICE LEVEL

RELEASE THE SPRING OF LIGHT WITHIN

4

- **Thought forms**

Thought forms are organic energies, have been created by the abundant information coming from the conscious and the sub-conscious. The conscious is the store everything learnt, heard and experienced during this life time on Earth. The sub-conscious is the warehouse for everything the soul went through since its existence. There are 2 more compartments of the mind need mentioning: The ego and the pineal gland. We are going to learn about them at a later stage.

Right now, let us get back to thoughts. In grammatical structure they are similar to sentences. In every thought there is a verb and a subject or object as the main stream. Depending on the emotional attachment usually colourful adjectives and adverbs are added to it. Every thought belongs to a cycle or a train of thoughts, I would say to the matrix of understanding in the mind. There are 2 types of thought forms: conscious and subconscious. Earthlings only understand and usually deal with the conscious ones. However, even modern medicine has some kind of understanding of the subconscious impulses coming from the *brain* they say. Since the sub-conscious is not tangible, it cannot be an active player in modern medicine. That is why it was named *sub* rather than *higher* or similar. On the other hand, even the most gullible spiritual stream calls it the Higher Self. Again, more about it later.

As I mentioned earlier, thoughts are organic energy. It means that they are alive and have the power to change their surroundings. As energies they have colour, smell, sound, taste and substance apart from frequency and speed. These are the readable data; I would call the knowledge of the thought.

Thought transmission and **mind reading** uses this phenomenon.

You have learnt that energies are interrelated. When we walk on a street, we interrelate with others who are passing by closely. When we sit next to someone, we exchange energies as everybody and everything is doing. However, nothing happens without reasons. The pull is between similar energies; therefore, your momentary ruling emotion would be drawn those alike. Sadness, hatred, anger, worry and fear are slow energies, and they would be drawn to slow energies in others. While joy, excitement, merriness and happy existence would attract those with same feelings.

Since you are the master of your thoughts, feelings, words and deeds, slowly but surely, you will learn how to recognize energies and how to manipulate them, especially your own, to make sure that you only pick up what you are looking for.

Occasionally happens that we enter a space, forced or otherwise, where the energies are noticeably different from that of ours. Discomfort sets in, and the only thought we would nurture is the idea of escaping from there. Sometimes we get irritated and at other occasions frustrated or even aggressive.

- **The life of a thought form**

At the instant of it forming a thought begins its life. It physically pops out of its owner's head and start looking for the subject or object mentioned. They look a bit like a caption balloons, carrying the words behind the energy. I call them sperms with their little tails looking for a place to settle. A thought's first aim is the subject or object about which, it has been created. The stronger the thought is, the better chance it has to reach its destination. However, on the road there are many obstacles it needs to overcome. The biggest is the cyber matrix from Wi-Fi, mobile phone connections and all kinds of chips we carry. These are very slow energies slowly destroying our existence and mess up our communication patters. It is a very broad subject we will touch upon later.

If the thought cannot reach its destination due to running out of energy or being caught somewhere, will look for an alternative place to settle. Being an organic energy, it is alive and needs to be fed. Taking the first similar energy mass is usually the safest alternative to finding the place it was originally destined for.

It is interesting to observe how a though eats you when it gets to you. Sometimes it looks impossible to get it out of your mind. While there, it makes alteration to the other thoughts you are nurturing: strengthens those alike and weakens the opposition. This is a good example of noshing.

Note

Let me give you another example: let's say you have a super strong thought about a person you really desire. We name him Dick. As the strength of a thought comes from the emotion behind it, this particular one will reach Dick. A desire, especially that of sexual nature, is a fire element, conveying high frequency energy; therefore, it needs a similar destination to hook into. For the sake of it, Dick is a fiery person with a lot of desire. Even if it is not towards you, the thought you created about him would land there and feed on his high energies and simultaneously nurture his. However, if Dick is not equipped to house the thought, it will look for another subject nearby. Misunderstandings? Sure.

Practice

Observe people around you. What do they think? Do they say what they think?

Apart from being great fun this exercise is one of the best intuition builders.

- **Ties**

We form ties with all the objects and subjects we come across, see, think of, talk or hear about. These ties are like threads between energies. The stronger the connection the thicker the thread is. The ties are seen by earthlings who mastered the craft of clairvoyance. Some animals who still possess the pure instinct would be able to see them too. Unfortunately, most pets do not belong to this category because their natural habitats were changed and they serve the needs of human beings more than co-exist with them.

These connections, as everything, are sometimes hindering, at others furthering the life of an earthling. Ties are only good if they help you with your path and unite for what you desire. Otherwise, they hold you back from learning, experiencing, evolving; in one word, living. They could prevent you from finding yourself and having your own opinion on matters.

A good spiritual understanding would advise you to cut ties with every thought and every organic energy, to free yourself and the subject or object concerned. A tie connects at least 2 things at all times even though one of them might not be aware of the link formed. It means that if you are longing for someone you are keeping that person on leash with your thoughts. The strength of the connection depends on the person's spiritual development; whether he is an independent thinker or not.

Note:

Ties are not always easy to recognize for we give them fancy names and importance. They are dependences we are anxious to have around or rely upon.

The most common ties are family, religion, education, social background, mass media and all sorts of material objects.

I do not mean that you should turn your back on anything mentioned above. However, you are only able to find your identity without the crutches, false security or an unidentified imaginary power looking over you.

To learn how to deal with ties is the biggest quest for earthlings. We need the material to protect and take care of our physical body; we need nurturing from time to time in our life and we also need guidance.

The mistake is that earthlings put people into compartments and treat them accordingly. The nearest to them generally is The Family. The people who are genetically related. However, within the family every soul has a path to follow and every one of them has reasons behind choosing that family. Since we do not talk about incarnation any longer, souls come from all over the universe to take on earthly studies. These are all experiences we gain through emotions. Although mass consciousness leads earthling to a uniformed understanding about family and life in general, earthlings are still individuals and have not arrived to the robot state yet. That is why members of the family are different despite of the same upbringing and education. We will talk about spiritual connections within the family at a later stage. Now I only wanted you to see the basic co-relations to enable you to look at your relatives as human beings and not as boxes entitled Dad, Mom, Aunt, and Sister and so on. Because that is what they are first of all. They have a life path to take care of and experiences to collect. I remind you here that being any of the above-mentioned family members is not part of the path. They are choices one might take on to ease or hinder life.

To be able to handle family situations you need to look at events from a human being's point of view rather than as a family member. Do not judge but learn them and do not have expectations towards them. Remember, they learn their roles just as you do.

The ties I am looking at are mental dependences. If you want to push your life ahead you need to get rid of these.

DISCOVER YOUR TIES MEDITATION

Discover your ties – meditation

Sit down comfortably with straight back and your feet on the ground. Go through the breathing harmonizing exercise.

For this meditation you need to ground yourself. Imagine that black roots are coming out of your sole and find their ways into the ground. You feel the cool healing energy of the soil. When your roots are established, invite the golden energy of the Universe through your Crown chakra. It has to be clear and sparkling golden. If it doesn't come at once, be patient and work on it, until you see and feel it in your mind.

With an inhale bring the light down to your heart chakra and release it in the front to form a path. Start walking on it. It is a cosmic path, suspended in the ether. You see the stars and planets around; you are out there as part of the whole.

As you walk, you see a 3-pointed star on the golden path, forming an obstacle. It is light blue in colour. Step into it and stay there until you become part of it by absorbing its colour. Continue the walk. Observe the space around. Next on your way you'll see a 4-pointed star that is dark blue in colour. Go through the same exercise and continue. The next obstacle will be a dark green 5-pointed star. After you see a light green 6 pointed, a red 7 pointed, a black 8 pointed, a pink 9 pointed and a lilac 10 pointed stars. Do the same exercise and continue your way until you arrive at a set of 7 steps going downwards.

As you arrive at the bottom of the steps, you'll see a great stretch of water, you might consider calling it *the sea*. Seat down into the warm sand and look at the water. Think about your life, particularly of your emotions. Get into the details and analyse them.

Suddenly you'll feel an urge to build a bonfire. Get up and look for wood on the beach. You will find good twigs around the palm trees. Gather them and produce a sparkle by rubbing two stones or pebbles together.

When the fire is burning nicely, gaze into the flame. As you do it, you will see all the people you are tied to and holding you back from your path. They do not do it intentionally and do not forget, that they are tied to you so they cannot follow their lives either. The connections are symbolized by threads. The thicker they are the stronger the dependency between the two of you. Burn those ties with the help of the flame.

Then you see the freed earthling dancing in the fire. You feel light and happy.

Everybody leaves the place. Extinguish the fire with some sand. Start walking up on the steps feeling the energy of each. When you reach the road make your way back. Go through each star again, all of which are golden now, and reach the place you started from: yourself.

Pull back the golden path, send it back to the universe with thanks, and pull your roots back. Thank mother Earth for the help and come back to your everyday existence.

Note

It is very important that you actually imagine [44] the whole journey as it is written to make it conscious.

Note your experiences in your journal.

- **More on karma, incarnation and reincarnation**

Places like Earth are good for awakenings. They offer different existences due to the needs and connections of the soul.

As I mentioned earlier, all our emotions are created by thoughts in the mind and generally run around the physical body. There are conscious and sub-conscious thoughts mirroring your momentary state of mind. The conscious thoughts come from the physical existence. They are important, for they show the evolutionary state of their master. Stronger attachments to the microcosm - that is the comfort zone, family traditions and religious fixations – relate to a lesser evolutionary state. Bearing in mind that the only freedom earthlings have is the freedom of thoughts, it is natural that enlightenment needs open horizon and flexible way of thinking.

None of the religions or fixed philosophies would take you to total enlightenment for they do not go with the flow and also restrict life. They denounce certain experiences and conceal existing channels between planes. Promises, hopes, easy ways and mythological backgrounds set back many Earthlings but those in search for true enlightenment would take on the bumpier road of learning and experiencing.

---

[44] Imagination is the astral projection of your thoughts.

Evolution of the mind and soul are the key points to karma and reincarnation for the state of mind mirrors the evolutionary level of the soul. I am not going to get deeper into evolution here as every bit of our teachings is about it.

Everything in the Universe is in constant motion and moves according to the laws of physics. Although they are given different names, metaphysics and quantum physics move on the laws of physics due to the fact that everything in the Universe is energy.

Karma is the debris of the interrelations of energy. It is always unsettled pulling power that keeps you back from the path you intend to walk on. Since it belongs to the past, it keeps you there. And if you are not in the present, future is very far away.

Karma is alive, for it is not finished. It is still in the energy field of the bearer, forming a dark spot that is visible for seers. The hue of dark and the size of the spot depends on the depth of the karma.

For clarification I divide karma into 2 groups:

1. Karma rolled over from the earthly life prior to this one.
2. Karma has been created during present existence.

The first group is the result of unfinished emotional events usually related to people from family, relationships or someone close. It could come from fear, anger, hate, deep sadness as the leftover of human interactions. These unsolved issues put weight on the soul and the earthling. Following the laws of physics, it is impossible for a heavy soul to break through and leave the magnetic shield of the planet, when at the end of its earthly life it passes over. Since the emotional distress happens through the physical body, the soul needs one to get rid of the karma. It can only happen through rebirth. The soul with karma, with the help of its guides, finds the best time and place to reincarnate into a family close to the other soul involved in the karma causing incident. New lives start to get rid of the weight and to evolve to the point when leaving the planet would not run into obstacles.

Note:

Since 14th of February 1972 only new souls come down to Earth. They do not have past lives here so rolled over karma is out of the question. From this time on every soul passing over is cleansed of karma and released into the Universe free. These actions are helping to speed up the planet and raise its vibration.

There are also souls who come down to Earth with an assignment or higher purpose[45]. Although they have lived on Earth before they are free of karma, for every time they pass over, the baggage collected during earthly life is taken off the soul. I call them incarnated earthlings.

The karma of the second group is much lighter, for it is collected as we live and evolve. Daily cleansing, stock taking, closures are the best tools for eliminating the slow energy particles, such as this type of karma, from our minds and lives.

---

[45] Every soul living on earth has a higher purpose. However, there are certain souls who need to work much harder to do the work they are assigned to do. If they do their work well, it would result in a big change in the lives on Earth.

Note:

We do online meditations and exercises to release the rolled over karma twice a year. Pay attention to our newsletter. This type of karma should only be released in the presence of a highly qualified master; otherwise, it could be quite dangerous. We will not be able to take responsibilities for your private attempts on this field.

EVERYDAY KARMA RELEASE MEDITATION

In Far-Eastern meditation exercises it is customary to sit on the floor with your base chakra touching the ground. It is because of the Kundalini energy they work with. Since our meditations are more astral travelling, we need different approach.

Like with every meditation we start with breathing to harmonize the chakras. Take deep breaths into the diaphragm slowly and release the air in the same rhythm. By inhaling slowly and down we take in a good amount of oxygen and by using the same pace we send the oxygen to every part of our body through the blood vessels.

For the better result we are not going to be rooted for this meditation. I am here to take care you on your journey.

Release everyday karma – the meditation

Sit down comfortably with your feet on the ground.

Invite the golden energy of the Universe to enter through your crown chakra and release it at the front through your heart chakra. The golden thread creates a road that is suspended in space.

As you start walking on it, you realize that at some points the path ceases but starts up again in the distance. These cuts represent the karma and what it does to your life.

With the power of your mind create a bridge between the two ends and continue walking. Repeat the exercise as many times as needed until finally you arrive at a 13 level steps going downwards. Every step has different colours. Make the first step slowly. Stay on it until you absorb its colour and become one with it. Listen to the sound around you. You guides are also talking to you. They remind you of your unfinished pull-backs. Take notes. Go through the same routine on every step.

At the bottom of the steps, you catch sight of a little wooden hut. Step in. Your guides are waiting for you. It is good time for a conversation with them while they are talking to you about your past. When they leave, thank them for the help and start working on solutions to all the events you have jotted down on the road. Forgive and release.

When you have done with the closure exercise, look around, open the door, step out and close the door behind you. Make your way back through the steps and the path that is now unbroken.

Get back to your everyday existence.

AKIA PHILOSOPHY®

APPRENTICE LEVEL

RELEASE THE SPRING OF LIGHT WITHIN

5

- **Life forms on Earth - what is out there**

From the momentary point of view, you need to know about 3 types of souls living in physical body down here. Later on we will elaborate on the wide range of the entire population; however now it is all we will talk about.

1. Reincarnated[46] souls

Earthly life was replanted at the beginning of the 1st Sun Age around 22.250 earthly years back. It means that there are souls who have been here for as many as a hundred lifetimes.

Due to the dense aura of the planet, here souls need a physical body to survive. Since the ozone layer doesn't allow energies through from the macrocosm, we need to gain life source from organic structures such as animals and vegetation. This is the point when the physical body becomes important. It houses the most elaborate chemical plant called the digestive system which processes the food we take in, hence make them digestible. Another important factory is the reproductive system. We will talk more about the physical body in the next level. Now you only need to know that reincarnation only happens because of this suit we are wearing. Think about it! Everything we do on Earth is connected to the body. We work, we eat we sleep and we become emotional due to its existence. And emotions are the factors of karma and heavy soul that result in coming back here once again for cleansing and solving unfinished businesses.

---

[46] Incarnation means to get into a physical body like the one we use on Earth. Reincarnation is a comeback straight after a life on Earth in order to conclude situations, clear up a left-over mass or release stuck emotions.

Like everything in the Universe, reincarnation follows the laws of physics. Initially every soul arrives here for one life time to learn and evolve. The physical body and the emotions attached to it are great teachers in understanding Earth, Water and Air elements and their interrelations.

When everything is cleared, emotional upheavals closed and lessons learnt, the soul loses the weight of worry, anger and sadness. It becomes fundamentally important when earthly life is nearing its end. Again, this event follows the laws of physics. When the soul is light in weight it can take longer journey from Earth by breaking out of the magnetic field. A totally cleansed soul has no bondage to the planet and able to go back to the place of its origin. If not, major cleansing is needed. In every religion and belief system there is some kind of purification to keep the soul light, and therefore fast, to break through the dense aura, the magnetic field of the planet and arrive back to the place it originates from. However, these methods, such as the Last Rite in Christianity, are not equipped to deal with the complexity of the laws of physics.

When the soul is not light enough to make the journey *home,* but not as heavy as to stay behind, will get into the outer aura of the planet we call the Shambala. On arrival there the soul would look through its life to see the milestones, hindering and furthering events and to draw conclusions from them. As their last duty in the life of the soul, the spirit guides[47] are there to help evaluate and make plans for the next descend. Apart from

---

[47] Every soul living on Earth has a set of two spirit guides. The help you connect, communicate even to make decision if asked. Christianity changed them into guardian angels. However, they do not guard but guide.

getting rid of karma, the soul will agree to perform some kind of service to the universe. That is what we call the life path. Considering these duties, the soul needs to choose the country and the family to born into. It is the time when the gender is decided also. It is vital, for gender determines the basic behaviour pattern of the soul and its views on the whole.

The prior objective is the karma. It means that if the other person who is connected to the karma is still on Earth, the soul is bound to find a place with close connection, in order to give the chance to both of them to clear the load. Sometimes the karma is carried to the Shambala by only one soul. Although initially it is *given* to two persons, one of them might have been able to clear it during the same lifetime. In this case the soul has wider possibilities to choose from, to support the second most important objective that is evolution. Before descend there would be a new agreement with a new set of spirit guides to match up to the next life.

2. Ghosts

If the load is heavy, powered by deep hatred, bitterness, anger or frustration the soul becomes overloaded by slow energies and will not be able to make the journey further than out of the physical body. These souls stay in between 2 planes, near the ground and sometimes they make certain earthlings' life miserable by appearing here and there, making strange noises and move object. We usually call them ghosts.

They are trapped within the physical plain. To remove the heavy load of karma they need to solve situations which connects them to other earthlings. However, this is only possible in a physical body. To get one, they need to reincarnate, and to do so they need to pass over properly. It is the situation when a ghost buster is more than welcome. Not the way they worked in films but a powerful lightworker would be able to raise the frequency of the floating energy mass to give it the well-deserved freedom.

Life path is always part of the evolution. One has to have certain knowledge to understand the value of the path, let alone walk it. Souls on the verge of reincarnating have pretty good idea of the rules, laws and regulations of earthly existence. As everything the information hinders and furthers their choices. Those with more courage and eager to take up a big chunk of the road to enlightenment would choose new and more difficult circumstances: like ethnic minority, poverty and even terminal illness to learn and teach. Others might want to take it a bit slower find a place with more certainty and structure. Both of those choices are lottery tickets. At the moment of birth, the soul *forgets* the task and all the contracts signed in the Shambala. Depending on the family, upbringing, religion, education and other factors, the new earthling will receive flashbacks and might remember bits and pieces. With education and versatile interests will obtain keywords to open files in the sub-conscious and gets nearer to The Knowledge that waits of discovery.

3. New Souls

The third category is the group of souls who are newcomers to Earth. They do not understand, and as the result, do not agree with all the man-made rules by which we are forced to live life. Since they are karma free from prior lives their auras have indigo hue that turns into silver from time to time. That is the reason why people started to talk about indigo children back in the 70s and after. Later the silver was explained as crystal, diamond and star seed, just to mention few names. The great majority of New Souls do not have fear for they somehow know that the Soul is immortal. The rest are very much afraid and retreat into depression type emotional disorder. This understanding is great help in my family counselling practice.

There is one more, tiny group of **Incarnated Souls** among us. They are workers who have certain duty to perform here, such as to bring important messages to earthlings, teaching something and also learn in the process. Many of the greatest minds are **Messengers**, such as Da Vinci, Bela Bartok or Tesla just to give you few examples. They do not enjoy privileges here, sometimes even pushed into hardship and struggle with life, to force into delivering the work they signed up to finish. However, society or the Mass Consciousness do not tolerate fundamental changes and new ideas, mainly for they are not understood and a revolution is always miles ahead of time.

Apart from souls, more and more robots are coming down to Earth. Their roles are significant. I will talk about them in a later stage.

Exercise

I remind you that souls born after the 28th of February 1972 are new souls and those born before are mainly reincarnated. According to this date you belong to either category.

Observe your ways of understanding and reactions. Compare them to the other group's behaviour pattern.

- **The light within**

Everything in the Universe is materia. As such, has structure, a chemical blend and physical data like speed, frequency, polarity, sound, smell, taste, colour and substance. Regardless of the data, every matter projects light of some kind; not all of which is visible by the naked eye.

As matter evolves, its statistics change. Evolution can go both ways: down or up. However, every change is evolution regardless the direction. On the way down the matter gets denser and the light it projects out would be smaller and darker; for it will have more Earth and Water elements in it. When evolution goes upwards, the matter gets lighter with Air and Fire elements.

Light is represented by the element of Fire. It depicts macrocosmic knowledge that help understand the Universe and the Self within. It filters in from the macrocosm, and based on the law of likes attract, it finds a sparkle to feed. The greater the sparkle the better the chance of connection. If the Light catches the ember in a dormant volcano, would result in eruption. Since the Galactic Quantum leap in 2012 C.E. the desire for connection strengthened and the macrocosmic fire is looking for possibilities to unite with the magma of the planet.

This motion results in a lot of disarray, such as earthquakes, floods and hurricanes.

As you remember, Fire depicts knowledge. That is why it is used in every religion, Shamanic work and healing in the form of bonfire and candles.

Now it is time to feed the sparkle within you, so you will never stop asking questions until the jigsaw puzzle of the Universe is complete and you will have a strong knowledge base to rely upon.

Time comes when you arrive at the understanding that everything happens for a reason and everybody always does the 100% of his/her abilities at every given moment. This realization will change your life.

I want you to use your intuition and figure out in which energy centre – chakra – the sparkle is within you. Name the chakra and let me know. I will tell you the truth. It is you first self-evaluation of the many to come.

AKIA PHILOSOPHY®

HEALER LEVEL

AKIA - HEALING

1

THANKSGIVING MEDITATION

The meditation – Thanksgiving

Please refer to your earlier studies.

- **Philosophy and healing**

It was only during the Pisces – Neptune era when sciences were divided and focused on microcosmic importance. Until then every field demanded the basic understanding of physics and mathematics as the essence of the Universal Matrix. Even literature carried its rhythm and carefully selected vowels strengthened the meaning of great works. Till that time healing was not considered a separate entity but part of the knowledge every human being carried. And it still is the part of functions we have the privilege to bear. We only need to remember and also through the philosophy it becomes natural part of living. I am aware that we talk about born healers and chosen people. However, as the founder and teacher of AKIA Philosophy and Healing Method I see that even the most scurpulous of my students would start remembering the art and successfully use it in everyday life. Philosophy and healing greatly compliment and help each other.

- **My consciousness**

My conscious esoteric career started when a then friend of mine asked me if I wanted to be initiated with REIKI 1. I was freshly back from Brazil for a short brake; full of the energy and wonders of South-America, where I had learned about energy healing and psychotronic[48], so I agreed. When I said I learnt, I meant that we exchanged ideas on these matters, for strangely I knew them all. I did not give names to these methods and I did not separate them. I have always understood that everything is interrelated and naming something would give it unqualified independence and ruin the Great Matrix of the Universe. That is actually one of the greatest conspiracies of lesser earthlings[49] towards the more developed or the totally gullible individuals[50].

It wasn't very long back but those days REIKI symbols were only available for people with prior initiation to keep the strength and also to protect those without understanding. However human beings are afraid of secrets. They take pleasure of infiltrating secret societies and powerful symbols to weaken them and sometimes even alter the path of understanding rather than learn their power and take in the Knowledge. This method is used to destroy the confidence in the Self, the

---

[48] Psychotronic is a fascinating healing method when the healer uses the psychic abilities of the patient and reflects it back to his/her conscious. This way the creation of new organs and healthy body parts take on a high possibility.

[49] As we are here on Earth to learn and evolve, lesser earthlings would be those who embrace the heavier elements, such as Earth, give into and promote consumerism, liquid money and all the other colourful bubbles that make peoples' life a misery. Individual power and gain are closely related to this lifestyle.

[50] Gullible people do not live but vegetate. They exist according to some kind of social agenda and they put a lot of effort into following them. It is also important that they do not develop individual dreams but take on the agenda without questions. These effects usually come from religious force or could be the result of laziness and lack of responsibility.

creative power we all possess and the strength of the Mind. As the consequence, the REIKI symbols are all over the net unguarded and powerless.

There is one more issue connected to most healing methods used. They float individually without a philosophy or a strong root. The latter is usually substituted by a story or as I would call, mythology to produce some kind of evidence of right or sustainability. In the case of REIKI, the story is that in the beginning of the 20th century c.e. Dr Usui, a Jesuit priest in Tokyo Japan, was asked by one of his students how Jesus was able to do all the miracles. The priest could not answer so he decided to leave the order and look for an explanation. According to the legend he wandered for 7 days without food and water. Finally, he gathered all his remaining strength and climbed up the nearby mountain to get nearer to God and begged him for answer and then in this hallucinating state he received the 3 symbols. He walked back to the monastery with his discovery and taught his students the secrets of the 3 symbols. Few years later he moved to the slum of the city and dedicated his life to the healing of the poor population.

I invite you to thoroughly research the story and tell me what is wrong with it.

REIKI symbols are Atlantean symbols used well for thousands of years for basic cleansing and sustaining health.

- **Political background**

At the dawn of the Age of Uranus – some might still call it the Age of Aquarius or the New Age - in the 1950s, a search for the Greater Good has started. Although the majority of the human race did not understand what the greater good symbolized but one thing was clear: nature had to be respected, the value of human life reassessed and after the 2 World Wars within a short period of time the strong desire for peaceful co-existence pushed earthlings towards spirituality. However, without understanding the true value of nature, respect is brought in by false appreciations and the lack of understanding the Self, made co-existence almost impossible.

Words like Freedom, Esoteric and Occult begun to circulate and opened the road to the teachings of great masters – mainly from Russia and Ancient Greece – also others from the Far-East, as much as to those set out to profit from the sudden demand on the market. Although we want to swing the responsibility on the politicians, the offer and demand on the marketplace is actually governed by the public. Nevertheless, the public is made up of individuals from different background, understanding and evolutionary state. Therefore, individual viewpoints and appreciation of life would mirror the intelligence [51] of the earthling in question. It is vital to understand that no one is more equipped to make decisions in your life than you are. Not even your parents, relations or teachers. You have to make the effort of seeing and implementing the information gained into your being.

Many of you might say: *why do I need to know about the political background when I want to learn a healing method? If I develop an interest in the matter, I can go to the history books and read.* Sure, you are right if you are satisfied with the surface information and not interested in the Knowledge. History books

---

[51] Intelligence is the level of global understanding. It has nothing to do with academic education.

are written by individuals from their own point of view and being re-written as we speak. Just a small example: Transylvania, the substantial part of the old Hungarian Empire was annexed to the freshly created (1861) country called Romania by the Trianon treaty in 1920. However, in Romania children are taught that Hungary was Romania and the old country occupied their land until it was given back to them. It is still the strong ground for the hatred between the 2 countries.

There is always a reason for everything. The example I have shown is a very common practice in modern time politics and between individuals; being applied on the weak and insecure at the most vulnerable time. Today this approach is used to conceal and destroy Knowledge. It is a psychological warfare that uses consumerism, including financial institutions and marketing to mislead the gullible.

Marketing strategies closely rely upon the above-mentioned phenomena. To satisfy those in power and the awakening earthlings, springs of esoteric knowledge were released; usually based upon philosophies like Buddhism, Hinduism and Taoism. Today the first 2 serve as religions, putting restrictions, rules and regulations on their followers. Surface Buddhism is widely used in Europe and North-America where people gather in temples and chant mantras of love and blessing without understanding the real meanings of words used. Cleverly it gives the momentary satisfaction of contribution to the flock and shifts responsibility to the rest of the population. It is also important to know that Buddhist are far from being peaceful. Monks are killing thousands of Rohingya Muslims in Myanmar and in most places, they get very annoyed if you dare leaving a temple without substantial donation. I spent a fortnight in Sri

Lanka recently. As a country it is nice and peaceful where religions do not collide and it was really good to see. Even the Tooth Temple where one of Buddha's teeth is kept, according to the guidebook, is set in the inner courtyard of a Hindu temple with the Christian church on its side. However, they became quite angry and verbal when we refused to donate after their answer to my question about the placement of the money was unacceptable.

I only mention Buddhism because it seems very fashionable today, especially amongst disappointed Christians.

Things changed since the awakening. Due to the poor understanding and decision-making abilities of earthlings a new religion emerged and a unified God has been pushed on the pedestal: MONEY. However, the Golden Era, which started with the quantum leap, supports and furthers the enlightenment. The choice is back to the individual.

REI – means great, sublime, royal; KI – is Chi, Qui, the life force. Later on it became known as Intelligent Energy for it is taught that the initiated, or as people in the United States of America say attuned, doesn't have to understand a lot about healing because REIKI energy knows where to go and how much of it is needed.

That was my first problem with REIKI teachings. Although everything is energy and as such carries a certain *knowledge* but it cannot think. With healing, constant decision making is needed and it is vital that the healer takes responsibility for his/her actions. I feel that REIKI teachings shift the accountability back to the Universe.

AKIA graduates are given all the opportunity to see the Universe as one and understand the role of the Self. We pick up the essence of teachings, clear them from fragile man–made extensions that do not fit into the matrix. We also provide roots and explanations. Since what is important is hidden, we trigger your mind towards questioning.

- **AKIA and REIKI**

Despite of its flaws REIKI teaching was and still is important for humanity. The basic course consisted of 4 levels with 4 symbols to correspond with the 4 basic elements of the Universe. It was pure, clear and great. Unfortunately, later on new levels and new symbols were added to fit the marketing strategy and it weakened the real value.

Here in AKIA, we teach the essence of the 4 original levels for the symbols are part of the Great Work, the Haya Sofia of Atlantis.

Practice

Write AKIA and REIKI separately on a piece of paper. Close your eyes and focus on the letters. Listen to your intuition. What does it say about these 2 words? What colours do you see or associate with them? What is the resonance of the letters?

VISITING THE SUN MEDITATION

The meditation – Visit the Sun.

Please refer to your earlier studies.

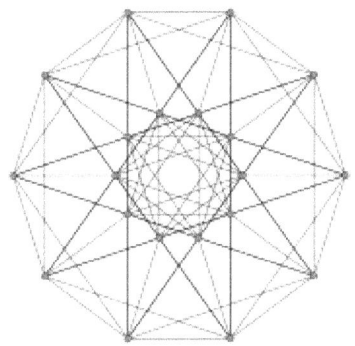

AKIA PHILOSOPHY®

HEALER LEVEL

AKIA - HEALING

2

THANKSGIVING MEDITAION

The meditation – Thanksgiving (ref: apprentice 1 page 7)

- **Blockages and residue**

Although REIKI has been categorized as a healing method its strength is in cleansing, relaxing and general maintenance of the body.

The physical body of an earthling is only capable of digesting organic energy. Non-organic energy intake remains undigested and produces residue that piles up and blocks the healthy flow of the life elixir in the body. With the wide spread varieties of ***genetically modified vegetables and fruits***, ***synthetic food products*** and ***codified soft drinks*** in the household, most of the residue and blockage derive from food. Since eating is the largest conscious energy intake, we are going to talk about it in depth later on. Subsequently you may refer to my book ***Heavenly nourishment*** published by ***AKIA Publishing.***

Another residue producing group is ***thoughts***. Some people and most studies say that we are not in control of the thoughts in our mind. I beg to differ.

Every impulse you have you form an opinion of even if you do not know. Probably that is why thought are considered uncontrollable. However, they travel between conscious and subconscious, also send a copy to the physical body through the thyroid gland. Thoughts are impulses that the body cannot take, so they are changed into chemicals by the thyroid gland and released into the system. Can you imagine?

We are going to learn about controlling the mind at a later stage. At this moment I would only like to add that thoughts are mainly responsible for the physical welfare of the body and the state of life.

Although they belong to the thoughts category, I would like to separate **karma and traditional behaviour patterns,** for getting rid of the blockages produced by them are far more difficult and delicate.

BEADBORD MEDITATION

The meditation – Beadboard   (Ref. Apprentice 2 page 10)

Practice

As you have learnt in previous lessons, it is vital to observe and take notes of your meditations and exercises in order to monitor improvements. Compare the results to all the noted ones and figure out why there are different. It is also time for you to use your intuition to bring meaning to the symbols in your chakras.

- **The segments**

It could be confusing to separate AKIA from REIKI teachings, since the basic practice of the latter is the part of the first. Therefore, I decided to add whatever I feel fit to build a strong base that you can rely upon in your development. These ideas would prove useful in your decision-making struggles and self-assessment practices throughout your earthly existence. You will still become a REIKI practitioner and if you feel determined enough you might even want to take on AKIA teaching.

In the Universe, even the smallest organic particle has 2 poles. One is stronger than the other at all time; however, in the case of healthy existence they alter by motions produced by the ups and downs of Life.

I'd like to note it here that mass media pushes earthlings towards monotony. Applying a good marketing strategy, they might call it **bliss, peace** or **harmony.** If you look at it carefully you would note that they are all names for vegetating and not living. It also happens because quantity is placed ahead of quality. We are guided to use our eyes only, and translate the received illusion into imaginary qualities that strengthen the floating bubble we call security. Do remember that important things are hidden!

Life represents constant movement that comes from the dance of the 2 poles. When in balance, the movement is reduced to mere necessities like breathing, eating and sleeping.

Let us get back to the segments. The smallest intelligent unit is a cell[52] with its 2 poles and the largest is the ever-expanding

---

[52] Mass of particles acting as a nucleus bounded by a wall.

Universe with its 2 poles. The 2 poles represent the opposite within the one, for without an opposite nothing has ground to exist.

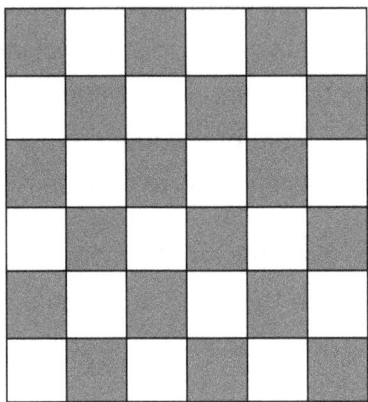

<u>Note</u>

This drawing is only an illustration that represent the harmony situation! The constant motion rearranges the cells at all times.

Every segment has an overall reigning polarity and 2 poles within; one on each side. Let us say that the red cells are + positive and the white ones are − negative. Depending on the quality of movements produced, the particles within a cell are rearranged, and that could result in the change of polarity. Sometimes the effect goes beyond the boundaries of the cell and spreads on the surrounding area.

I want to emphasize again, that positive and negative are polarities and have nothing to do with the often-used terms. They cannot be translated as good or bad for every good carries bad and every bad has good in it. It is also important to understand that we judge events through a filter which is the mirror of our momentary point of view.

REIKI teaching puts great emphasis on polarity of the body. Nevertheless, it follows the Far-Eastern understanding of static and unchangeable qualities, according to which the physical body is divided into the 2 poles that is determined by the gender. Since there is no evidence to support the theory that the left side of all females are positive and the right is negative, in AKIA healing, the polarity of the patient as an energy mass is important regardless of the gender. We also put emphasis on the local polarity of particular parts or organs of the body for illnesses produce different polarities. As an example, inflammations and tumours are positive in polarity therefore negative energy is used for the treatment. The directions of the energy flow differ according to polarity, so do the person's mental approaches to ideas and questions. It is like favouring one particular side of a street. Both take you to the same place but one of them feels more comfortable than the other. Have you ever wondered about why is that?

Exercise

As an exercise, observe your walking habits. Alter them and note your feelings about it. As you walk imagine what is happening behind the walls.

- **The function of the chakras**

They are vortex-like junctions of energy flows. According to general polarity of the person, or I could say the bodies of the earthling, energy lines would take a certain turn at the meeting point that would determine the way the chakra moves. The root chakra of an earthling with negative polarity would turn anticlockwise while the other with positive would make the same journey clockwise. Chakras are segments, positive follows negative so the next one, the sex chakra would take on the opposite direction, and so on.

Crown ↪

Third eye →

Forehead ↪

Throat ↩

Heart ↪

Solar Plexus ↩

Sex

Root

Chakra turning of an earthling with negative polarity. The third eye shares the forehead and it acts as the channel to the Universe.

Crown

Third eye

Forehead

Throat

Heart

Solar Plexus

Sex

Root

The chakra turning of a person with positive polarity.

- **Individual chakra cleansing**

To get rid of the blockages on a daily basis is a real good preventive way of looking after the welfare of an earthling. Chakras are the gates to the outside world and they should be kept clear at all time.

All healing and cleansing happen on the spiritual body. In the case of distant healing the astral body is invited to work with. However, at the beginning of our practice we are going to disregard these facts.

Reiki is usually practiced on a massage table where the patient is laid down on his back first. Following your intuition decide the polarity of the patient. DO NOT WORRY IF YOU MAKE A MISTAKE! Apart from a slight headache and light dizziness nothing would happen if you slip. However, it is a good way to start trusting yourself. This will be vital not only in your healing work but in every corner of your life. Harmonize the energy flow by making large circular movement above the body if your patient is lying down. The direction of circles should correspond with the turning of the root chakra for the individual you are treating. Again, you need to trust your intuition to do efficient harmonizing. Then make a spoon from your palm by closing and curving your fingers. Allocate the root chakra and with a circular movement spoon out the residue. I advise you not to touch the body but work 6 inches (15 cm) above it.

Note

Healing is a conscious psychic work where the trust of the Self is vital. Everything you do with your mind and motions you need to *see* happening. One might call it imagination but one cannot imagine anything what is not there. Therefore, when you spoon the residue out you feel the weight of it in your palm and feel its substance on your fingers. This way your actions will have a beginning and an end. Residues are slow energies therefore we cannot just release them into the Universe. As you know, similar energies like each other and the blockage would end up in the energy field of someone with some kind of slow energy like anger, sadness or illness and would result in a *when it rains it pours* phenomena. Teachings usually assume that nature can recycle the residue. However, it is far from the truth. Look at nature how polluted it became from the rubbish dumped into it. In AKIA we use the creative power of the thoughts to turn the unwanted slow energy into gold. Gold is a symbol of pure knowledge, fire element and the Sun. It also depicts the fastest energy available. To turn slow energy into gold is easy; you just snap your fingers and imagine the action. My students use this motion because I do. The strength is in the coding. Whatever the motion is, it has to be associated with your action, therefore you need to focus on it in your mind to encode the certain motion you decide to use. Snapping fingers is good because you use your hands in the cleansing and healing.

Cleansing a chakra usually takes more than one spooning. Do it as many times as needed. You spoon – pull – snap and spoon – pull – snap. When you are satisfied with the cleansing procedure you need to accelerate the energy centre by using your hand and make fast circular movements in the chakra. The direction of the move should follow the turning of the particular chakra. In the case of negative polarity, the root should be turned anticlockwise. Now you need to fill it with the most beautiful golden energy of the Universe. As you have been doing it in earlier practices, imagine the brightest golden light coming down from the Universe and let it flow in through your crown chakra. You feel the warmth as it descends into your hear centre. Follow its way into your arm – whichever you use for healing – and it comes out on your palm chakra that is in the centre of your palm. Hold your hand over the energy centre needs to be filled and let the energy flow. Use your intuition to stop it whenever you are satisfied with the result. Do not worry, you cannot overfill a chakra. When you finished you go onto the next centre.

Spoon – pull – snap, spoon – pull – snap, spoon – pull – snap – whirl - fill

Use every opportunity to observe. Not with your physical sight but with all the other senses you have. Touch energies and feel the difference. Imagine their colours. Bear in mind that a human being is not capable of imagining what is not there. Terms like fantasy and imagination were created at the beginning of the Pisces era, about 2,200 years back, when spiritual knowledge was pushed back and the so-called reality took over. However, what is reality?

When you finished with all the 7 chakras you turn your patient over and do the same on the back. After, you do 7 soothing motions from head to toe and release the person. Experience shows that laying the patient down is only for the treated person not for the healing itself. It could perfectly work if you call the earthling's spiritual body if he is nearby, or the astral if he is further away. The spiritual body works within 60 feet (20 m) radius. Then imagine the person being in front of you and locate his root chakra. It doesn't have to be at the real height; your mind needs to believe that it is there where your hand is working.

Although everybody should be really grateful for your efforts, there might be people who will get irritated by the sudden cleanness and the free flow of energies. These earthlings are used to slow energies and usually reconciled to some kind of suffering or ill treatments. They are afraid to take responsibility of their lives and like to vegetate rather than live. We might say *let them do it, it is their lives.* But we live in co-existence and their energies affect us. Therefore, with patience we should work on altering their energy level to save our own.

Not everyone is lucky enough to have many people willing to help with the experiment and practice. If it is the case, do not despair. Just invite the astral body of the person and do the same thing on it. To invite an astral body is easy. You think of the person clearly and say it in your mind that you want his/her astral body to come. However, you can only do it for practice purposes. You cannot possible do it for personal gain. Also, there is a very important law in the Universe that nobody should be treated or healed who doesn't seek help. It means that asking for help is a virtue that people need to learn.

Nobody should take others for granted and you should not walk around *helping* people to boost your ego. However, in this time of your studies practice is needed, so the law can be pushed aside.

Exercise

Offer you service to people around and watch their reaction. Write your experience into your journal.

Note

Healing is a conscious work that needs sharp senses and mind. Every soul living in a physical body is capable of healing. There are no chosen ones or born healers. Some people might carry the knowledge nearer to the surface and they remember easier but with open mind and willingness everybody can get there. It is a given gift to humanity. Do not forget, we are equal.

VISITING THE SUN MEDITATION

The meditation – Visit the Sun.

Please refer to your earlier studies.

AKIA PHILOSOPHY®

HEALER LEVEL

AKIA – HEALING

3

THANKSGIVING MEDITATION

The meditation – Thanksgiving

Please refer to your earlier studies.

- **Atlantis**

As we go along, I will throw piles of information in front of you. Some of you would say *great, now I understand it!* And other would say *what a crap!* Or *I don't know what to do with it at this point!* Or you might decide to give credit to everything I say without questions. I cannot really tell you which is the best way of pursuing your studies for we all are different. I would suggest that you question but do not doubt. Instead of saying *I do not believe,* you might want to say *"Why?"* And *"How?"* One thing I promise: If you are open minded and intelligent enough, one day it will all make a lot of sense. Since **AKIA is the philosophy of the unseen soul and cosmic knowledge** more and more hidden value will surface and information becomes knowledge.

According to my research Atlantis has never submerged into the ocean. Evidence shows that the great majority of modern Brazil, almost all of Mexico, the Caribbean Islands and Bermuda formed parts of the land called Toreos that was renamed Atlantis at a much later stage.

The first 144 souls, *dressed* in physical bodies descended to Toreos at the beginning of the 1st Sun Age in B.C.E. (before Common Era) 20,238, to start up a new cycle of earthly existence yet again.

I stop here for one second. It would be much easier to say this sentence in person so I could answer all your questions. However, it is not possible so I assume the questions you might want to ask.

There are 2 official theories in circulation about creation. Although totally different, they seem to go hand in hand. Everybody on Earth is familiar with the Christian theory of creation. And due to the effort of the Catholic Church the story filtered into other religions. However, be reasonable! How could God create the world, when it/he/she had already existed? Who created it/him/her? How it/he/she was able to form chemical substances to fit into the surroundings physically? What it/she/he created the Universe from? Nothing? How can anything be created from nothing? On the other hand, as the second theory, in the education system, the same people, who carry this religious belief, teach Darwin's evolution. Being a freemason, Darwin had a substantial understanding of the Universe. The only mistake he made is to link vegetation with animals and animals with human beings. This approach was also adopted by Far-Eastern philosophies and religions where earthlings, animals and vegetation are interchanged in the reincarnation process. One thing should be clear: nothing happens in vain and everything is a consequence of something; events are interrelated.

Let me just conclude with two sentences here. My understanding always follows the laws of physics, without which there would be no existence of any kind.

It is also important to understand that nobody is punishing you for your deeds but you do it yourself. What comes around goes around until you learn your lessons. This phenomenon and everything else in the Universe solely follow the laws of physics. Without it the matrix of the Universe would fall apart and disappear into the abyss. Ideas and theories which do not fit into this category should be dismissed at all times.

- **Sun Ages**

To understand what a Sun Age is you need to refer back to your prior studies. When I say 1st Sun Age, it doesn't mean that there was none before. However, from the earthlings' point of view it was the very first in this cycle. The Mayan calendar shares my approach. They talked about the 5 Sun Ages and they were able to put the exact date on the Galactic Quantum Leap on the 28th of December 2012, on the Full Moon and the Winter Solstice. It was a translating error and religious belief that ended up with the 21st of December 2012 in the media, for the Common Era began much later than the Mayan Calendar; nevertheless, people seem to fixate on the 21st of December for it already bears some kind of importance in the Common Era calendar.

According to the Maya the 5 Sun Ages are as follows:

1. b.c.e. 20,238 – b.c.e. 16,230. The 4,008 years was the time of Water was named Matlactli Atl that means 10 waters. During this time giants lived on Earth who fed on water corn. At the end of the Sun Age water purified the planet, people turned into fish and only 1 couple survived.
2. b.c.e. 16,230 – b.c.e. 12,220. The 4,010 years was the time of the water serpent called Ehecoatl. People fed on

a fruit called acotzintli. Ehecoatl ended the era. People turned into monkeys and again, only 1 pair survived.
3. b.c.e. 12,220 – b.c.e. 8,139. Tleyquyahuillo was the name of the 4,081 years. People ate the fruit called tzincoacoc. Fire finished this Sun Age.
4. b.c.e. 8,139 – b.c.e. 3,113. The 5,026 years was called Tzontlilic. This was the time of Blood and Fire. As the result of a big fire everybody vanished.
5. b.c.e. – 3,113 – C.E. 2012. The era was governed by the Sun God called Tonatiuh. At the end the planet moves and everybody dies.

As you can see, they understood a lot but their belief system wasn't free of fear. Remember, fear sets in as a filler to seal the gaps where knowledge cannot reach. At the end of each Sun Age a quantum leap happens which involves the whole solar system. Through experiences and learning, planets leap into a higher evolutionary level, inhabitants included. This event is symbolized in the Mayan calendar with the clear cut of everybody perishes and the new life is ensured by the surviving couple.

The 5 Sun Ages made up a cycle and ended in a Galactic Quantum Leap when the whole galaxy leaped up one evolutionary level.

Note

We usually perceive improvement through the eyes as a quantity rather than a quality. By sharpening your senses, you will be able to see the hidden values behind events and will understand that improvement cannot come from continuous joy nor from sturdy disappointment. Use the first to gain strength for the next lesson and the latter for evaluation of your thoughts.

- **Precession of the equinoxes**

There are many people out there who talk about the Age of Aquarius. Some think it is due to arrive 30-40 years' time and others would say it is even further into the future. I haven't met anybody yet who would say it is already with us. Perhaps because the expectations are high on the changes produced by the event. The shift in energies constitutes modifications and presents us with hope only until it is in the future. Nevertheless, the truth is that the dawn of the shift started around the 1950s and resulted in freedom movements, spiritual openness, emotional growth, artistic development and the embrace of the new. As the consequence a desperate attempt to control was pushed ahead from the opposite pole.

- **How the change happens?**

Earth spins anti-clockwise around its axis that is tilted by 23.50 degrees. The tilt derives from the pulling power of the Moon to make the axis perpendicular to her equator. A whole spin takes one Earth-day. Also anticlockwise, Earth travels around the Sun. It orbits the "master" on an ellipsis. On this ecliptic - equally 30° from each other, although not at the same height - are the 12-star formations of the zodiac. During its orbit Earth pays a visit to each star formation and spends equal time in the court of all.

Do not forget that the sky is not a 2-dimensional colouring book! When I say Earth visits, it is only a figure of speech! This period comes to more or less a month. The whole circle takes a bit less than a year. Over 2,160 years these bits add up to 30° degrees on the ecliptic, meaning that in every 2.160 years Earth slips back one constellation on the orbit therefore the Sun rises in the court of a different constellation when the Spring Equinox appears. Naturally the connection between our planet and the Sun is changing accordingly. The key date is the Spring Equinox. The constellation where the Sun rises - on the end of March Full Moon, at the time of the Spring Equinox, would bear a significant effect on the lives of Earthlings therefore we call it the ruling constellation.

Since Earth slowed down significantly during the past 160 years due to the residue, karma and blockages earthlings recycle into it, the ecliptic shortened, the effect of the 12-star formations disappeared and the ruling planets took their places. In 2003 Neptune energy was conquered by the now reigning Uranus. The fast, feminine, high frequency energy is responsible for the shifts and created the era we call the New Age.

Note

At the beginning of the 1st Sun Age Earth was aligned with the 22-star formations zodiac. Venus only entered the Solar system after the 4th Sun Age around 3,113 b.c.e.

C.E. 2,003 –   Uranus

b.c.e. 157 – C.E. 2,003	Neptune - Pisces
b.c.e. 2,317 – b.c.e. 157	Mars - Aries
b.c.e. 4,477 – b.c.e. 2,317	Venus - Taurus
b.c.e. 6,637 – b.c.e. 4,477	Mercury - Gemini
b.c.e. 8,797 – b.c.e. 6,637	Moon - Cancer
b.c.e. 10,957 – b.c.e. 8,797	Sun - Leo
b.c.e. 13,117 – b.c.e. 10,957	Mercury - Virgo
b.c.e. 15,277 – b.c.e. 13,117	Libra
b.c.e. 17,437 – b.c.e. 15,277	Pluto - Scorpio
b.c.e. 19,597 – b.c.e. 17,437	Jupiter - Sagittarius
b.c.e. 21,757 – b.c.e. 19,597	Saturn - Capricorn
b.c.e. 23,917 – b.c.e. 21,757	Uranus

As you can see the end of the 5th Sun Age coincides with the finish of the other great astronomical cycle: the precession of the equinoxes. We are going to learn more about the astronomical influences at a later stage.

After the Galactic Quantum Leap, we entered into the Golden Era that lifted the planet out of the Dark and being influences by the Light and the Knowledge. Naturally it doesn't mean that everything is honky dory now. Although the planet survived the Galactic Quantum leap but it triggered the opposition to work harder on destroying it.

VISIT THE SUN MEDITATION

The meditation – Visit the Sun

Please refer to your earlier studies.

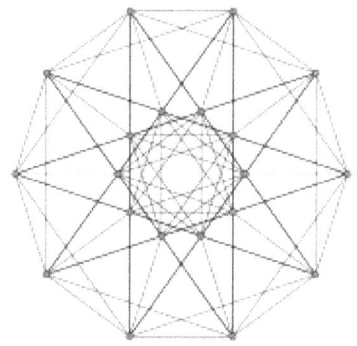

AKIA PHILOSOPHY®

HEALER LEVEL

AKIA – HEALING

4

IN YOUR TEMPLE MEDITATION

The meditation – In your temple

Light one basic white candle and an incense. The candle has to be scentless, white and without metal holder. The incense can be any kind of burning stick, sage or frank incense. It is not advisable to use any other type of so-called purifier, because they are coded for different scenario and approach. Stick to tools mentioned in your learning material.

Sit down comfortably with your back straightened and feet on the ground. Imagine a golden beam of Universal Light to descend on the top of your head. Open your crown chakra and let the Light in. As you inhale the Light descends further down into your body until it reaches the end of the bone between your ribs. This is the place people usually call 'the gut'. It is your Solar Plexus. Now imagine that the Light finds its way to flow out of your body at that point, where it draws a golden path, the yellow brick road into the infinite distance. You start walking on this road. Do not be afraid of anything and anybody. Remember, you are within yourself so if you meet anybody or see anything they are messages from yourself to you. Pay attention!

You see a meadow in the distance. Walk through it until you arrive at a dwelling of some kind: it could be a castle or a hut. Open the door and step in. Your spirit guides are waiting for you there. Sense them. Get familiar with them.

There is a door on your right, take it. The staircase leads one flight down where you find 2 doors. Open the one opposite the stairs. The room is dark with some light filtering into it through the drawn curtain. Walk to the window and open it. Gradually the room is forming shape in front of your eyes. You see pieces of dusty furniture, things scattered as if someone left in a hurry; dust particles are floating in the light and the air is stale. Open the window and breathe in the fresh air coming through it.

There is another door on the landing, just next to room you are in. It is full of cleaning material and furniture. Pick up what you need and clean the room thoroughly. Fashion the room the way you feel comfortable with. It is your safe haven, the place you can retreat to anytime you need to think, plan or decide.

As you clean rugs, carpets textiles are merging from drawers and wardrobes.

When you finished you take a shower in your bathroom and whip up some party food in the kitchen. Invite everybody you wish to see or talk to.

Note

This place is on the astral level and whatever happens there, would be conveyed by the astral bodies to the person they belong to. It is also a good place to tell people things you are reluctant to do on the physical plane.

I realize that I repeat myself from time to time. Experience shows that it works out well for students.

Thank everyone for coming and let them go. Clean up the place yet again; close the door and walk up on the steps. Your guides are still there visibly happy with the progress you made. Listen to what they say.

Say farewell to them and step out of the place. Close the door behind you and start walking back on the same road you came. When you reach 'yourself' pull the Light back into your body, let it flow out of your head and release it into the Universe. Say thanks for the Light.

Your experience should be noted in your journal.

- **The symbols**

As I have mentioned earlier, we recognize only the basic 4 symbols in REIKI teachings for they are part of the Torean heritage. The rest have been added to live up to expectation of the market rather than help the learning and healing process.

Before you are initiated into the knowledge you need to be attuned to the symbols in order to make learning easier and more successful. Also, to give you adequate protection against unwanted energy flowing through the opened chakras. An open gate is a two-ways street. Although it is possible to close down the communication for one way, it would be totally unacceptable from the learning and evolving process of the earthling concerned. Without courage, experiment and experience, the body, mind and spirit cannot get ready for spiritual work and life itself.

As your educator and esoteric master, it is my duty to take utmost care of your well-being. It means that I never put you into excessive danger but push you to limits in order to develop your protective senses and open your horizon.

It is also important to understand that in healing we are instruments for the energies of the Universe. By taking care of the mind, the body gets ready to filter in selective energies and guide them to places of need. We are not healers really but allow the Universe to use our faculties to do its best to trigger the self-healing process in earthlings. We all carry the physical requirements of a healer. However, the work needs to be conscious and guided by the mind.

- **Getting attuned**

With this exercise you need to connect to the logo yet again. It works as a channel between you and me. I am the one doing the attuning that you receive via the AKIA logo. To connect please refer to earlier exercises.

Before connecting you need to perform a cleansing meditation. Please choose the one connected to the Sun to fill yourself with its golden light.

AKIA-HEALER ATTUNING MEDITATION

The meditation – AKIA-HEALER attuning

After sufficient cleansing you continue sitting there with straight back, your chakras aligned. Bring in the golden light of the Universe through the crown chakra and bring it down into the heart chakra. Imagine that the energy beam divides into 2 streams: one flows into the left arm and the other into the right one. They stop when reached the palm chakra in the centre of your palm. Feel the warmth of the light tickling your palm and spread into your fingers. Keep your eyes closed and feel that I draw 3 equal legged crosses on your palm chakras. Put your palms together to allow the energy form a circle and flow freely in your body. Separate your palms, pull back the golden light and release it into the Universe. Before thanking for it, feel that I draw 3 equal legged crosses into your crown chakra also.

Thank the Universe for the light and come back to your physical existence. Now you are ready to talk about, work with and touch the symbols. However, talking is limited to your fellow practitioners.

SHO KU REI

This symbol is the magnet, connected to Earth element.

Physically strengthens the energy received from the Universe.

Before any kind of healing work or for physical boost you draw the symbol into the air 3 times. It would open the fast track between you and the Universe.

Good for physical up-lifting of people and places

This feature is very useful when you have a meeting with someone who is of slow energy; or you need to go to a similar place such as medical centre, tax office, bank or any kind of government building. In case of a person, imagine that you have his astral body in front of you and draw the symbol on it 3 times. When you enter the building, you do the same.

In circumstances when you are not alone and drawing into the air would bring undesired attention, you say the name of the symbol 3 times and imagine it.

Draw on the organ being healed

When you self-heal or heal a particular organ, you may draw the symbol on it 3 times. As it is a laying on of hands healing, the choice is yours whether you want to touch the body or hover your hand above it. For some wishers-to-be-well touching is a necessity for it carries psychological substance.
This practice helps even with the highest level of healing beyond REIKI.

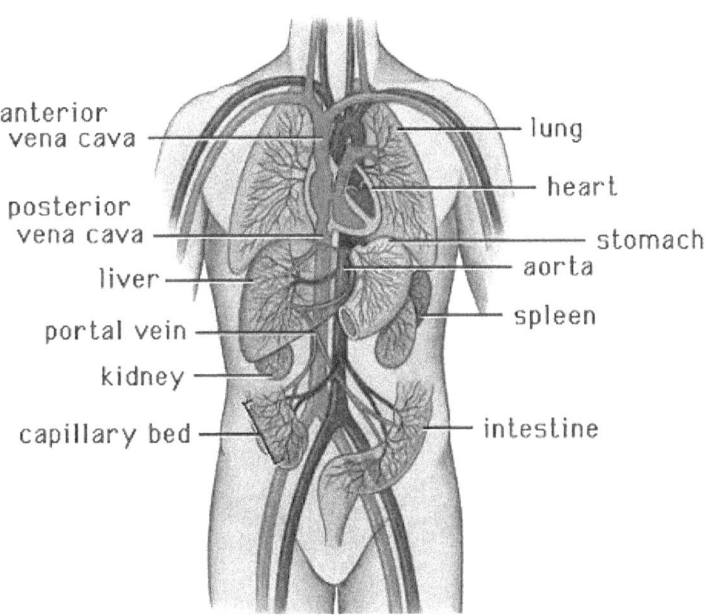

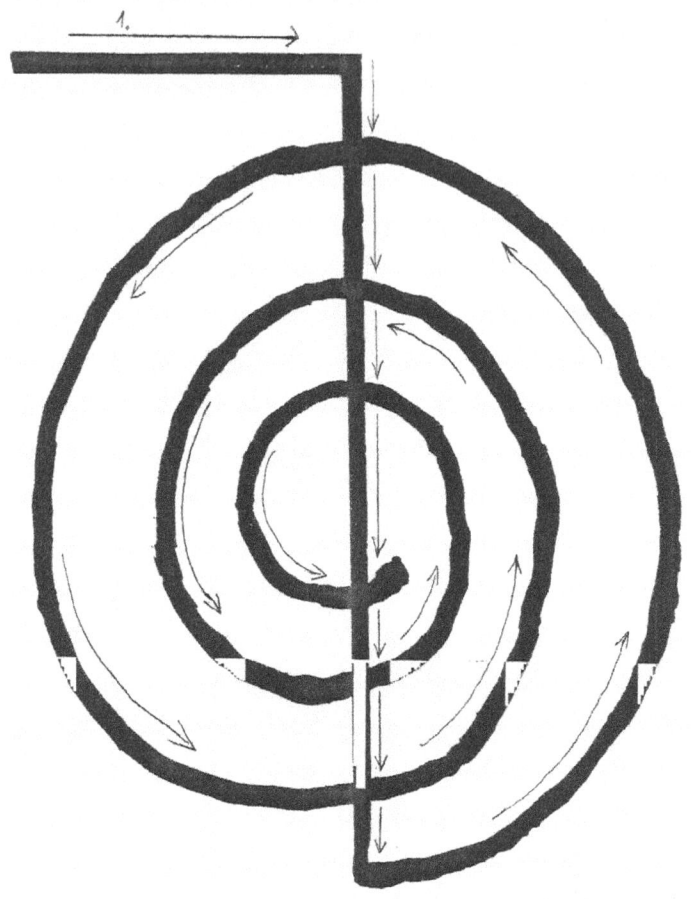

SHO KU REI

Raises the energy level of food by removing unwanted substances

This is one of the most important features related to this symbol. We are presented with a lot of artificial food nowadays. The industry is genetically manipulating the products to be more desirable, addictive and thought altering. With the simple use of this symbol, you can eliminate undesired man-made additions to food products. Keep it in the kitchen drawer and put a sign on the food on the table.

Do not forget, symbols need to be hidden from those not attuned!

Removes side effects from medication

Although we are learning about the self – healing capability of the body and mind, there are earthling who turn to medication for comfort or out of desperation. At this point Sho Ku Rei will help get rid of the side effects and undesired chemical substances in the medication prescribed by a medical practitioner. Again, draw the symbol on the medicine before taking.

Note

Modern medicine is one of the greatest conspiracies against humanity. It has been designed to treat the symptom and not the illness and genetically manipulate earthlings. **Natural remedies** however support the physical body and could be used successfully without artificially added chemicals. That is why the law is tightening around the use of natural remedies, herbs and various healing methods. Vaccines are slowly becoming compulsory so nobody can escape the grip.

AKIA PHILOSOPHY®

HEALER LEVEL

AKIA – HEALER

5

THANKSGIVING MEDITATION

The meditation – Thanksgiving

Please refer back to your earlier studies.

SEI HE KI

This symbol is a magnet related to Water element.

Lifts depression

As the most lucrative result of the New World Order, depression became the state of mind in the White Peoples' Land, such as Europe and North America with the United States and Canada. It is an axiomatic that earthlings coming from so called less civilized and poorer places in the search of fortune and wealth, will fall victims to this brain washing bubble industry human beings of the mentioned lands are forced into. It might be a strong statement, for nobody is holding a gun to our head to accept certain situations; however, events walk hand in hand. First of all we need to look at the word **civilization**. Through education and media, earthlings led to believe that civilization means material wealth and high technology around the household. But the Greeks had a very different view of the word they invented. They looked at it as an organized and caring society with high cultural and social structure, within which everybody equally benefited from free education, medical care and cultural development, all of which need emotional presence. By now, the meaning of the word slimmed down to **organized**. The added values are **capitalist**, therefore individual, centred on tangible material and surface behaviour; **ignorant**, we forgot to read and write, perform simple equations; **insensitive**, people are killing each other without reasons and we don't really bother as long as the chosen side is doing it to the rest of the world. Culture, such as literature, poetry, painting and high value acting, is slowly demolished and emotions are secondary citizens in the lives of earthlings. Since what is really important is hidden, we float on the surface in various bubbles conveniently called **security**, **protection** and **freedom**; we spend a vast amount of our free time to take care of these bubbles and shorten the road between them in order to preserve the protection by shutting out new impulses in every way possible.

The bubbles we live in changes our view of life. What we call security is permanence, protection comes from systems bought to take care of the first bubble, and freedom? Well, it is something we have less and less. With the internet and mobile phones your whereabouts is to be known and seen by many. Social media giants work with authorities of different kinds to track you down and look at every move you make. In many places, such as the European Community, new rules are born each day to tighten the boundaries and narrow the minds of its citizens.

One might say that we need rules to abide for safety and security purposes; however, everything has two sides. Only robots can follow this kind of order. Human beings are individual, they come from different places as souls, carry special experiences and above all, have feelings. Emotions which are created in the mind triggered by effects and counter effects, fear, insecurity and confidence. Although brainwashing is popular and intense, the mind is free. It cannot be forced into a cage. When there is an attempt, the mind retreats into a place where it is permitted to fly and crush man – created boundaries. Society might say that *he lives in the world of his own*. Sure, he does. It is a lonely world with events he has no courage to initiate in physical reality and appreciations he cannot see possible elsewhere.

Depression could also come from mere laziness that actually is the lack of life elixir; the drive keeps us on the road to be challenged constantly. Sometimes the loss of someone or something invites depression in, when the loss is so unbearable that shutting oneself out of life seems the only solution.

Since AKIA philosophy® is a complex and comes with a very good healing method, as a student you need to know that depression comes from an enzyme manufactured by the kidney, it becomes apparent that the responsible energy centre is the root chakra and the main causes of the illness are the ties and feelings related to material and organic energies such as animals and human beings. As a secondary cause I would mention rules and regulations, belief systems and misconceptions about existence as a whole.

There is only one way out of depression and it is willpower. Although guidance is necessary but if you refuse to embrace the changes and decide to vegetate instead of living, the chances of improvement is rather slim. Modern medicine might bring smile on your face but the reality would not change. SEI HE KI is a good way to help in this kind of need.

Ask the wisher-to-be-well to draw a picture of his life he wants to arrive at. Pay attention to every little detail. The key words are strength and belief here. One might say that you need fantasy for this exercise. However, as you have already learnt, fantasy is stretching your thoughts and one cannot see or imagine something not being there. Obviously, if you cannot imagine a better or I would prefer a good life for yourself, you are not going to get there for you do not allow yourself this privilege.

Let us get back to the picture of the future. It has to be clear, well composed, doubtless and without mishaps. There should never be plan A and plan B. All your strength should be focused on one attempt. Words such as *if, maybe, perhaps and only* have to be forgotten. Bear in mind that you are the therapist, the guide here. Without putting your thoughts or ideas into the picture you need to make sure that the one created has potentials and show the best ever outcome of the situation. If it is not, your client needs to go back to work on the future. When you are satisfied with it, tell him to hang onto the end result and you draw the SEI HE KI symbol 3 x on the point where the scull meets the spine on the back of your head. This way you lend strength to the idea and chisel it into the conscious of your patient. The practice with SEI HE KI bears great responsibility. It is something as a healer you need to learn. Do not be frightened; believe in yourself and the power of healing.

Note

Security, protection and physical freedom are illusions. They simply do not exist. Think about it. Every fence, security code and protection can be broken into or might just be faulty. The interrelations of energies are stronger than any of the man-made structures.

Alters sadness

Sadness is the result of clinging into certain thoughts which make you a bit lost and insecure. By applying the symbol on the temple, you speed up the exchange of thoughts and give ways to new, healthier ideas.

Helps with emotions

Emotions come from the mind as the result of the thoughts cultivated there. Sorting out the mind would make emotions more understandable and easier to deal with.

Draw the symbol on the forehead chakra 3 x and breathe deep. Let it help see the whole picture.

Clears thoughts

You might want to delete certain thoughts from your mind. Again, draw the symbol on the forehead and let it do the work for you.

Note

In self-healing you project your spiritual body in front of you and do the work on it. Mind altering could be tiring for the self. However, if you are capable of changing the picture of your life, you are most definitely ready for a new beginning.

PROJECT YOUR AIMS INTO REALITY MEDITATION

The meditation – Project your aims into reality

Start your meditation with deep breathing following the rhythm of one-two-three-in and one-two-three-out. Do it 5 times.

Invite the golden light of the universe through your crown chakra and let it settle down in your heart. From there, release it on the front to draw the road. Start walking on it. Think about your aim. See the end result in its full glory. Do not be shy and do not hold yourself back. Believe in your capabilities and strength.

As you walk the yellow brick road plan the first step you need to accomplish to put your aim into reality. See yourself making that step. The result should appear in front of you with the glory or further questions. The latter needs to be addressed and should create the next step on the road. It is up to you how far you want to see your goal to develop. Fear would hold you back but courage might make you big headed. None of them is good, for you need a logical view of step-by-step actions.

As you are getting further into the projection see yourself in the event with all the possible outcome of your actions.

When finished, start walking back. Pull back the road and send it back to the universe with thanks. Come back to your everyday existence.

Note

Change is the most important factor of life for it produces emotions what is needed as a fuel to push the machinery ahead. It can be in anything. Bring in new cereal, hold your teacup in the other hand, change your route to the bus stop or just walk on the other side of the street. Observe your feelings while doing them. Take on the excitement of the new rather than the annoyance.

Select an aim for the day while having your coffee or tea. Every single day should have something. You might want to call it the Change of the Day. Then you need to figure out the first step towards this change. It will start the Plan of the Change.

Miracle Box, praying, mantras and any other kind of non-physical, therefore idle deeds should be pushed aside. It is your life and everything in it is your responsibility. However, you need to be reasonable. Asking for a Cadillac would only bring result if you had the money on your bank account to purchase it. Love would only come if you were ready for it and searching.

"God,

Give me the Serenity

To accept the things, I cannot change.

Courage to change the things I can

And Wisdom always to see the difference."

Note

Do not forget to put your projection into physical reality!

VISIT THE SUN MEDITATION

The meditation – Visit the Sun

Please refer to your earlier studies.

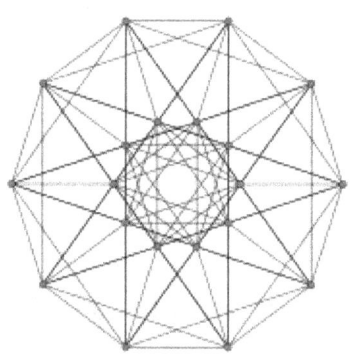

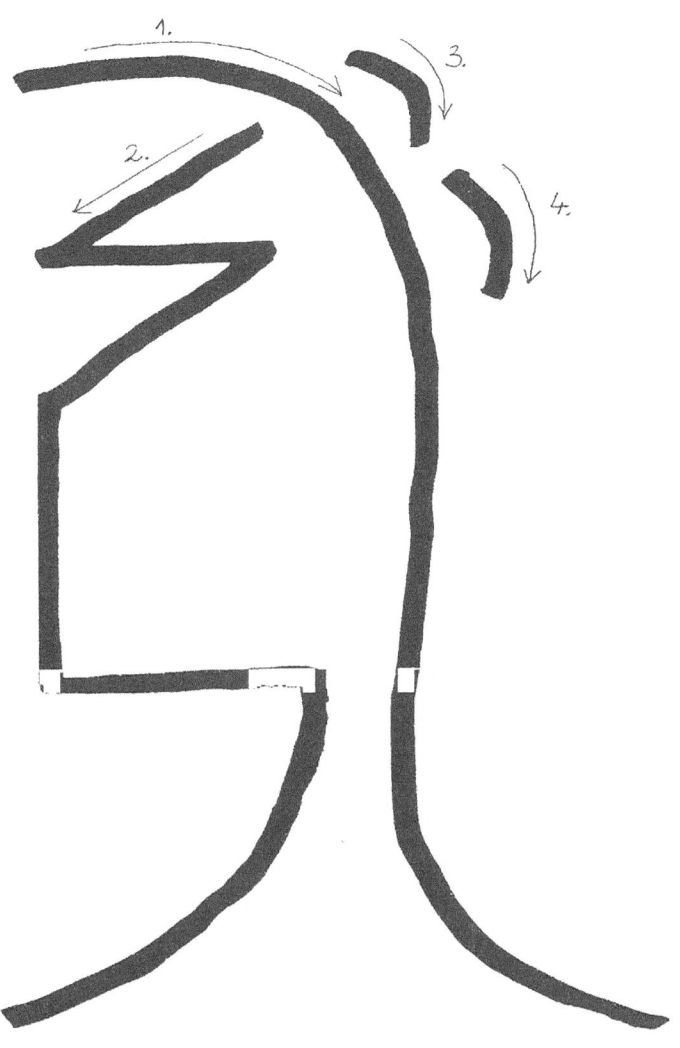

SEI HE KI

AKIA PHILOSOPHY®

HEALER LEVEL

AKIA – HEALING

6

BEADBOARD MEDITATION

The meditation – The Beadboard

Please refer to your earlier studies.

HON SHA SE SHO NEN

This symbol is a magnet working with Air element

Excellent for distant healing

As you master the understanding of energies and the belief in their power, your strength would take you on the road of distant healing. Basically, REIKI is a distant healing method for there is a gap between the hand and the body; however, if the wisher-to-be-well is present, the practitioner can work with the spiritual body which carries the healing to the physical body. Even though one might not have a sharp enough seeing ability, there is always another body between you and the patient in his physical reality. The physical body is not capable to take on this strong and selected beam of healing power. When the patient is further away, like in another city, country or continent HON SHA SE SHO NEN proves extremely useful. In this case the astral body is invited to take the healing, for the bond between the spiritual and the physical body is very strong and the leash is short.

In this case you draw this symbol first and then add any other one you feel fit. Invite the astral body of the patient. If you cannot see, imagine it being in front of you and work on it accordingly. You do not need to move up and down, just say to yourself: *I am working on the root chakra now, or I am cleansing the kidney now* and your thoughts would connect the energy with the body part.

Raises the energy level of places and events in the future

Distance is not only relevant to place. It goes into the future as far and as near as you want. HON SHA SE SHO NEN programs situations and healings for the desired time.

Let us presume that you want to do some healing for someone on the East coast of the United States and you happened to be in England. As we established earlier the astral body needs to be invited to you as it is able to travel and its absence would not damage the owner. However, when the 3 bodies are not together earthlings weaken and their mind gets scattered. The degree of the change depends on the knowledge of the being and its capability to deal with the situation. That is why the healer needs to pay attention to the habits of the patient. Time zones are important too. In the case I mentioned earlier your patient will be 5 hours behind you in time. The safest time for distant healing is when your wisher-to-be-well is safely at home, sitting down or already comfortably in bed. This way weakness would not cause upheavals. The 11 p.m. bedtime there would give you 4 a.m. next morning what probably isn't the best time for you to focus. With the help of this symbol, you can perform the healing a day to one week earlier at your chosen time.

After the necessary preparation you decide upon the time and day for the healing to reach the patient. Do not forget, it has to be his time and day! Write the date and time on a piece of paper to make it conscious. Add, that you are preparing a healing to be sent at this particular time. Invite the astral body. Draw the symbol 3 times on it. Heal.

Sometimes one occasion is not enough for the good work. With the symbol you can have repetitive healing for up to a week. Add your request to the time and date. Although you do not need to work with it during the given time, it is useful to put a note into your diary just to keep it in mind.

Distant healing takes about 3 – 4 days to bring an effect. Ask for feedback when the time passed.

Although we call ourselves healers, we are channels for the energy that heals and it is our duty to keep the channel fit at all time. That is why genuine healers understand that you not only can but should help others only if you are in a pretty good shape concerning your understanding, responsibilities and aims in life. A weekend course, regardless of its price, would not make you an instant healer. It is a never-ending road where you heal yourself to enable the capabilities within. Remembering what is said you have to perform a good cleansing of your energy centres in order to get rid of the blockages and residues in your body. Choose one of the cleansing methods you have already learnt. It is advisable to light a white candle and burn an incense while working.

Good self-healing tool

Self-healing follows the rules of distant healing, but invite your own astral body for the process.

EXPAND YOUR AURA MEDITATION

The meditation – Expand your aura

Sit down comfortably with your feet on the ground. Straighten your back to allow the energy to flow.

<u>Connect with the logo.</u>

Get into a slow rhythm of inhaling and exhaling. One-two-three-in, one-two-three-out.

Invite the golden energy of pure Knowledge and Light through the crown chakra. As you inhale bring the light down to the root chakra and fill it up. Then bring it down to the sex chakra and fill all of them one by one with the golden light. Keep inhaling and let it spread all over your body. When your toenails are golden and your hair shines of the light, as the extension of the body, your aura will receive the surplus. Let it be. Feel it expanding with the dense energy. As your golden aura fills the room you start feeling light footed. It grows out of the house and the street while you are floating higher and higher above the ground. You see the street under you getting smaller. Houses and people are covered with the golden light and are filled with high frequency healing energy of the universe.

Pay attention to staying in control all the time. When you start distancing yourself from physical reality it is time to come back.

Slowly release the light back to the Universe through the crown chakra and arrive back to your physical existence. Thank for the light and write down your experience.

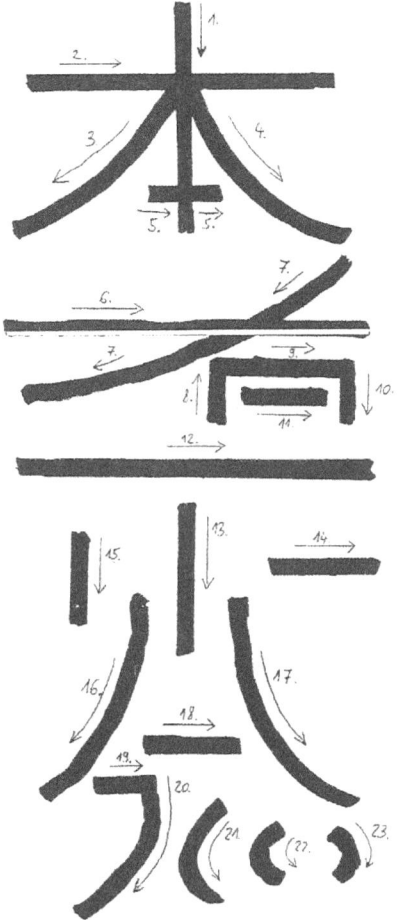

HON SHA SE SHO NEN

VISIT THE SUN MEDITATION

The meditation – Visit the Sun

Please refer to your earlier studies.

AKIA PHILOSOPHY®

HEALER LEVEL

WATER INITIATION

1

BEADBOARD MEDITATION

The meditation – The Beadboard

VISIT THE SUN MEDITATION

The meditation – Visit the Sun

- **Becoming an earthling**

In the Keta School of the Universe the soul needs to be transferred into an earthling through understanding the magnetic bond what keeps it earth bounded and the rules and regulations come with earthly existence. Since the star gateway opening in 1972 reincarnation stopped and only new souls are allowed to come here. The necessary requirement of becoming an earthling is a physical body. It serves as a digestive and reproductive system and also as the tool for learning and evolving. However, it is also a prison with limited moving potential and there are no multiple entries once it is chosen as destination for a soul. Everything we do and feel here is connected to the physical body one way or another. It is the life-time dwelling for the soul-earthling.

Keta School is open to souls who want to experience and learn. When the journey is decided, the soul looks for a physical body to *get into* to suit its goals and learning procedure. Social background, ethnic group, continent, country, gender and genetic inheritance are important issues to decide upon. However not every physical body is taken by souls. Social requirements are pushing people to reproduce, mainly to ensure the continuity of consumerism and the payment of unfulfilled loans. As the consequence more and more *empty* physical bodies are amongst us functioning in a robot-like state. These *people* are easily swayed and used by sweet talkers, powers or authorities. The soul-less bodies provide excellent hide-away for temporary observers from other planets on a learning mission.

Despite of the common belief, extra-terrestrial life forms are not necessarily more advanced than that of earthlings. From the universe's point of view technical development serves as disruption, for it eliminates organic energies without which life ceases. At this moment we focus on souls in a human form who lived without physical body or as different life forms in the Universe prior to descending here. The information and knowledge, gained during these existences, is stored in the subconscious; forming the filter through which they observe this strangely unique place. For reincarnated souls familiarities become déjà vu-s but new events bring frustration.

New souls have two extreme options in handling Keta. Either to be courageous and bold to thrive on challenges and adventures or withdraw from life completely and vegetate in deep depression. However, the great majority is working in the space between. From the evolutionary point of view every event has to be treated as an experience: learn and draw conclusions from, through the observation of the 2 poles.

There is also an event we cannot leave untouched. As the zodiac of the 12-star formations was travelling out of alignment and the New Age approached, pre-written destinies opened up; giving choices to individual earthlings to evolve faster and to heal Earth by getting rid of the heavy karma of the past. The intention is excellent, the help from the Universe is ample and infinite, but earthlings do not seem to be ready to handle so much freedom and decision making that suddenly became available for them. It is the greatest paradox of earthly existence. All earthlings want is freedom: to be happy, healthy, and successful, usually with plenty of money, and do it all with the least commitment and headache possible. Then, when opportunity knocks, confusion and frustration set in. Without proper knowledge about the interrelations of energies choices cannot be made and fear mirrors the ignorance of the individual. **It happens because the only freedom exists and possible is the freedom of thoughts.** The very thing we are so willingly giving up for ideas and guidance from the man-made POWER: MONEY.

Have you ever asked what money was? It is mysterious, untouchable and therefore valueless energy. It is the newly created God that exists above everything and as all the others, an invisible illusion that exists in everything. It is there, floating in the air as a reminder that no other God exists, for all religions surrender to it. Ironically it is the God of the only religion which unites Earthlings. The faith is called **Consumerism.** Seemingly it supports the kind of happiness everybody pursues, and the illusion that it could be bought, hovers overhead. In the chase it is difficult to see that people are killed and nations are wiped out in support of the new belief system.

But real happiness is not available for everybody; it needs to be earned by conscious work for it comes from within and as a philosophy, it will change the way you look at the universe and yourself. AKIA shows you the way. Follow the step-by-step instructions and exercises until one day you wake up and realize that the Light was born in your Mind and the jigsaw puzzle is solved. Like in every school, learning is easier for some and harder for others, depending on the filter of the mind. Airy belief systems which do not form part of the matrix, would take one into a cul-de-sac without offering the possibility of a U-turn. Nevertheless, all religions say that we are created by God as the multiplication of itself. Therefore, we need to understand God, meaning the first Knowledge that was able to multiply by division, to get to the real Self. Here is some guidance from the great mind of Hermes Trismegistos:

> *"If then you do not make yourself equal to God, you cannot apprehend God, for like is known by like. Leap clear of all that is corporeal, and make yourself grow to a like expanse with that greatness which is beyond all measure; rise up above all time and become eternal; then you will apprehend God. Think that for you nothing is impossible; deem that you are too immortal, and that you are able to grasp all things in your thought, to know every craft and every science; find yourself home in the haunts of every living creature; make yourself higher than all heights and lower than all depths; bring together in yourself all opposites of quality: heat and cold, dryness and fluidity; think that you are everywhere at once, on land and at sea, in heaven; thing that you are not yet begotten, that you are in the womb, that you are young, that you are old, that you have died, they you are in the world beyond the grave; grasp in your thoughts all this at once, all*

times and places, all substances and qualities and magnitudes together; then you can apprehend God. But if you shut up your soul in your body, and abase yourself, and say: "I know nothing, I can do nothing, I am afraid of earth and sea, I cannot mount to heaven; I do not know what I was, nor what I shall be", then what have you to do with God? For it is the height of Evil not to know God. But to be capable of knowing God, and to wish and hope to know It, is the road which leads straight to the Good..."

As I mentioned earlier, there is a path to follow. Depending on the individual filter, one is inclined to take either of the following ways. Sometimes it is necessary to mention things more than once.

1. <u>The way of the Fakir</u>

It is a long, painful and uncertain way which focuses on the physical body and earthly existence. He stands motionless for long, tortures himself with fire or nails and never takes anything without physical suffering. On the road he develops a strong willpower but there is nothing to aim it towards, for emotionally and intellectually he is undeveloped. This group of earthlings is called **Hylic**, for they represent the materia, the non-organic.

2. <u>The Monk</u>

He has a deep religious conviction and belief. His life does not go beyond the boundaries of religious rules and sacrifice, while he is working towards some kind of reward that is promised to him. The life of a monk is a chain of suffering with emotions he needs to control and deny. Finally, he will understand emotions, but his body remains basic and his way of thinking will remain within the narrow boundaries of his conviction. This group is called the **Psychic** for they work on conquering and eliminating emotions.

Note

Please understand that the real meaning of the word has nothing to do with certain abilities people may have or not.

3. <u>The Magus</u>

He seeks Knowledge and Understanding of the interrelations of energies. It is the way of the Mind; the embrace of the Conscious and Subconscious, the Two Poles, Sun and Moon, Light and Dark. It is the way of Knowing. However, this road is not possible without the experiences gained from the two previous ways. This group represent the collective consciousness of the **Spiritual**, where through experiences earthlings work on understanding the interrelations between events.

As a student of **AKIA,** you are taken towards the third path. On this road one needs to be very alert to find hidden and belittled values. When musical masterpieces like Puccini's Nessun Dorma is used to advertise a meaningless timewasting serial like Party Down South; candles and incense are called esoteric; the person who understand all your whims is your soul mate; someone who learns tarot reading from a book is called psychic; the Eye of Horus is known as the symbol of Freemasonry and Alchemy is considered to derive from Jewish mysticism, well there is a lot to search and dig for. Patience and logic are needed to find morsels of the Real Essence before it all disappears under the haughty castles of the New World Order.

Note

Although I take you on the third way, I definitely do not want you to give up living. I rather urge you to dive into it, take responsibilities for the Self, learn your place in the Universe and take action to make it better. Knowledge is only valuable if you can put it into action. Then it becomes Wisdom.

- **Emotions**

Emotions are the machinery of life. Without them an earthling stops living and deteriorates into the abyss of passing. However, passing is not as easy as we might think. It takes many years of subdued refusal of going with the flow, to interrelate and to be part of this magnificent learning procedure we call life.

As everything, emotions also come from the mind. It is very naïve to think that we catch them from open air or even better, we are chosen by them; and if we are not careful enough, they torment us for years to come. I am only saying it because in my family and relationship counselling business people are talking about, *I cannot help it*. You know, when we say, oh yes, I am in love with him. I cannot help it. He is nasty to me, he beats me up, but love is blind. Not at all! Love is not blind but we are!

We have certain preconception about everything, related behaviour patterns, all kinds of do-s and do not-s; some of which we learn watching our parents and the grown-ups around. A big portion of these fixed ideas would come from the media such as films, music and magazines and what we might refer to as education. There is also religion to concern and should not forget the inclination of the soul according to the knowledge to which it has access.

With this foundation life starts and interrelations begin. Everything we do, think or say is energy; as they interrelate, they generate emotions in the mind.

It is vital to provide experiences for young earthlings from a very early stage to trigger the brain. Without events the senses would sit idle and there would be no impulses to start the thinking procedure. Generally, people pay less attention to their children than they spend on pets. A dog needs to be walked at least twice a day with patience while you let it sniff everything on the road, stops or runs according to its feelings; on the other hand, children are shuffled into cars or pushchairs and have no contact with the world around; while parents fiddle with Facebook or have meaningless conversations with someone on the phone. The touching, sniffing and tasting experiments of a child are usually cut short by overcautious parents.

As we grow and go through experiences in life, the emotions generated by interactions will change. A type of joke you found hilarious last year might not bring smile on your face this year. Events and interactions of your own, continuously influencing your ideas of issues.

The emotional state of an earthling changes by experience and knowledge. When I say knowledge I mean the Haya Sophia, the Magnum Opus, the knowledge of the Universe. Naturally it is a choice to pursue the Knowledge, or struggle through life.

Emotions are the mirrors of the manner how one looks at the world. Now you might say that there are people who successfully conceal emotions. We describe nations with words *cool as a cucumber* and there seem to be an etiquette code according to which we prejudge people.

Think about it! We do not trust one who smiles a lot or laughs, thinking that he is not trustworthy and serious.

Imagine, whatever we do it comes from our emotions, and emotions come from whatever we do.

- **More about chakras**

This is the place where everything happens. It is the meeting point of the 3 bodies – the astral, the spiritual and the physical – where thoughts and experiences are exchanged. It is the bridge between the conscious and the subconscious. Furthermore, it is the place where the macrocosmic triangle touches the microcosmic one and if circumstances permit, they start slipping into each other by narrowing the gap between the two planes. This action is controlled by the trinity of the eyes. The left eye is Water, subconscious and positive; the right is Earth, conscious and negative in polarity; the third eye is the neutral one, blending the two viewpoints and creating the momentary Knowledge of the earthling with help from Light as the conveyor of cosmic experiences. This knowledge makes up the energy mass of the soul. It is the result of a very complex information exchange brought in by the senses.

As I mentioned earlier, we only focus with one eye at every given time according to the initial viewpoint we stored in the brain. Using the right eye, we would be looking for a so-called realistic view while the left gives us some room for improvement. However, regardless of which eye we use the information received would end up in two places at the same time: in the subconscious and in the conscious.

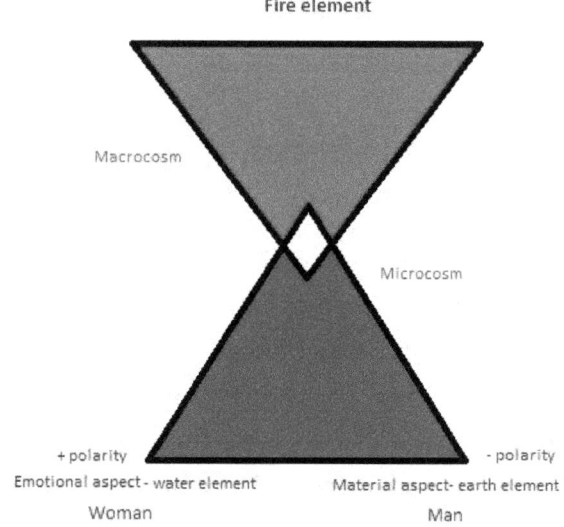

The third eye or the neutral eye is called by different names to fit philosophies or religions: God's eye, the eye that sees everything or it is preceded by the name of a certain prophet. I like the idea of ancient Egypt and usually call it the eye of Horus for it fits the trinity structure of the Universe: Isis, Osiris and Horus. Also, the Eye of Horus, like everything else from the same place is designed according to the function of the pathway. Therefore, the eye has 6 doors. They are assigned to the senses where impulses and information come in. It mirrors the evolutionary state of the soul with the hindering and forwarding behaviour patterns and thought forms. I also favour it for the fact that it is the most ancient and significant.

- **Code**

I do not support the idea that we carry a code from our earthly ancestors. These codes are supposed to lead you to the trodden path of your grandparents, in some cases that of your great-great grandparents. They are also meant to transfer or continue the responsibility for their deeds onto your shoulders creating quite an upheaval and many obstacles in your life. When we look at the constantly moving Universe, we realize that this idea is only wishful thinking by those who dislike change and dwell in the past. Or of those who want to implant fear and with that total succumb to man-made controlling rules. It is a very dangerous idea indeed. The foundation is quite fragile and totally dismisses the possibility of the Macrocosm by turning Earthlings into narrow minded robot-like creatures with very few choices about the future.

The code was invented and supported by the New World Order. Its purpose is two tiered: 1. it supports the latency of earthlings by creating a pre-written and non-changeable life path to succumb to and 2. it shifts the responsibility of loan and mortgage payments from parents to children. You might say that law supports the inheritance of assets also. However, this way children are stuck with properties they might not want, forced to live in a certain place, carry particular lifestyle that seem to be predestined but might not be desired. This way migration slows down and consumerism is assured.

Earthly ancestors mean very little to the soul. Many people follow or relive the life of a parent of the same gender believing that there is no choice; that this path has to be taken for it is karmic or simply fate. Well choices do not come to you by themselves. One needs to have adequate information to be presented with choices. Everybody has a choice but one needs to find those paths. For many people having choices is a curse. Different aspects need to be looked at and decisions have to be made. The other convincing feature of path-following is fear.

There are certain cases when one follows the footsteps of a parent without much thought and consideration; when reality hits it is too late to stop the motion. Looking at parents as raw models can make or break the future of a child. There is far more to parenting than staying together and pretending to be a happy family. We are going to talk more about this issue at a later stage of the study.

There are also physical inclinations such as certain movements and ways of carrying oneself; likes and dislikes for food, drink, events and so on. As likes and dislikes are in the mind, I would not take it as a code. My parents divorced when I was 4 years old. I lived with my mother who was constantly blaming my father for everything and spread nasty stories about him even though she was already remarried and had a new baby from the second marriage. One day, when I was eating sourcrout, which happened to be my very favourite dish, she mentioned that I was a lot like my father because I loved the dish and so did, he. I put the spoon down straight away and had not look at a sour cabbage dish for a couple years until I had the opportunity to meet my father and understand him a bit better. I realized that he was not a bad person so it stopped bothering me that I favoured the same dish.

Biological inclinations are very tricky indeed. The physical body is the merge of 2 other bodies therefore there is a great possibility to develop dispositions towards certain illnesses or other inclinations carried by one of the merging bodies.

These tendencies are dormant until a key energy trigger them open. And here we arrive back to the interrelations of energies for it is the key to everything. Depending on the relationship between the conscious and the subconscious one carries a certain emotional state which works like a magnet and pulls in certain energies to interfere with the condition of the existing one. This way inclinations open and blend into the life of the unsuspecting victim.

It is vital to be able to look at your parents as human beings. As such, none of them is *perfect* for it doesn't exist. You need to allow them to make mistakes and understand that they do not stop living a path only because they chose to parent. On the other hand, as the child, you are not allowed to be irresponsible and waiting for your parents to clean up the mess behind you. As an earthling you should be observed and treated by relatives.

As a healer I would say that these inheritable tendencies are not only detectable but curable. Now I let you on a secret I use for healing the case. Everything important to an earthling is in the mind. Therefore, the mind enjoys special protection from intruders and slow energies. I grouped up brain functions and created 12 cells that are easy to handle and good to work with during healing. For extra protection I put those cells into the *merkaba*. It is a *spaceship* for the soul we use during astral travelling and also serves as a protection for life functions. The door of the merkaba only opens for the owner. Every soul has a merkaba however one has to be ready to work with it. Naturally you will learn about it later.

Everything we do here on Earth is about the interrelation of energies in human relationships. These experiences further the understanding of the Self, the 4 elements within and around, and the journey towards the ultimate goal: the connection to the Creator force within. Without it the Fire element of the Universe would go unnoticed and wasted. It is the condition to become the part of the whole and to find the *balance* we seemingly seek.

As my experience shows this harmony or balance is widely misunderstood amongst earthlings. Out of the few goals we aim for this is the most common. We never stop dreaming about it; however, deeds usually stay in the background or begin an unrelated journey. We have been fed with fairy tales which show the struggle we need to go through to reach the "and lived happily ever after" state and it is always the consequence of marriage, if I put it loosely, a couplehood between 2 different gendered healthy earthlings with some sort of wealth behind them to support the harmony they are after. This is a symbolic view of earthly living and should not be taken word by word. The "what is important is hidden" theory is in action here once again. The wedding of the 2 poles means that the interrelations are learnt, emotions understood and mastered, and the 2 cosms are united in one within one individual. With the 4 elements alive, the earthling is ready for evolution and the quantum leap. This is the marriage we are after; in reality however, the meaning is concealed behind dogmas, spiritual and religious views that mirror the actual evolutionary level of their creator.

The "live happily ever after" concept depicts an imaginary state earthlings search for. "I only want to be happy! Is it too much to ask for?" we say while waiting for some kind of a miracle to provide us with the subject or object of our happiness. We do not realize that the question itself is the only obstacle that prevents us from reaching a state of fulfilment. Primarily the sentence is pointed to the Self, and quite rightly I must admit, for happiness comes from within, whatever our understanding of the word is. Nevertheless, we mislead ourselves by pretending to be aware of this. On the picture behind the question there is always somebody taking up a very prominent place in the outcome. Why do we say "I want to be happy" when it is conditioned on the presence and motions of another person? There are 2 answers to this question: we either do not care about the feelings of the fellow earthling in question or we do not understand that mutual consideration is needed. Neither of these conditions takes us closer to the goal due to the lack of a basic understanding of earthly living.

Earthlings are here to evolve through experience. Basically, there are 2 kinds of experiences: conscious and subconscious.

Although they both further the journey, in this case I talk about spiritual experience and not of money-making skills, earthlings who are aware of the path set their goals with an understanding that aims are only necessary for drawing the initial direction and enjoy the ride. Subconscious experiences are thrown in by the Universe to help the evolutionary journey. As everything is interrelated these events are actually the consequences of the energy movements in one's life. Earthlings who are spiritually aware would be grateful for and learn from both. Others would get angry, depressed, hurt and unhappy about the subconscious experiences, and would hurry to reach the goal they consciously set without walking the path towards it.

It does not matter which way I look at the interrelation of energies in human relationships, the Self has to be built in order to understand that you are responsible for not only your deeds, words and thoughts but for those of every human being because you are also affected by their deeds, words and thoughts.

It is very easy to get lost on the road to fulfilment. However, one thing is for sure: there is no easy way and spiritual development is a must. The fear of being different keeps a lot of people away from this search and the misconception concerning the meaning of spirituality and religion only add to the task load.

A religion is a set of beliefs and practices often centred upon specific supernatural and moral claims about reality. It shows the highest level of existence and convinces you that you can never get there. Becoming part of a religious group only requires acceptance of the mentioned beliefs; while spirituality is an individual and sometimes lonely path to walk in order to become one with the Creator Force.

Looking at our world at the moment there are different groups trying to push, sometimes even force earthlings into agreement with their theories of life by limiting the views of the Universe and promising salvation for deeds they consider proper for a human being. Needless to say, the choice is yours. Occasionally one might be forced into joining certain assemblies but the real and the only freedom dwells in the mind regardless of the behaviour pattern of the physical body.

Religious groups and individuals who denounce the exchange of energies between earthlings in any way, are hiding away from the pleasure, sorrow, happiness, sadness and the other feelings encountered through this type of exchange. As practice shows, their aura is pale and the fire is missing from it altogether. One might say that being connected to the Creator Force is all one needs, and that knowledge finds a way to flow into the consciousness of the individual. However, we are here to learn and go through certain events and to understand the Creator – meaning the first knowledge that was able to multiply by division – within. Without this wisdom one cannot get connected to it, due to the dividend created between the 2 worlds. It is all physics: the Creator force is a high frequency energy and you can only reach it by bringing yourself up to that state of Knowledge.

Coming down here is usually an evolutionary choice. Turning away from earthly life by hiding behind dogmas and excuses to spare the self from hurt, disappointment and sorrow work against the purpose of life. It also prevents the soul to taste the wonderful experiences of everyday events. Living in physical body but putting the maintenance of it on the shoulders of fellow earthlings is an unfair deed. Even if these fellow earthlings are your parents or siblings. The proper aim is to learn to support yourself and break free. Modern religious groups, especially those embracing the surface understanding of Far Eastern philosophies, get what they want from others by using the most common black mailing system of shifting responsibilities and raising guilt in the uncertain and undecided minds. They might even say what they do is a sacrifice and that it is done for the benefit of humanity. Do not be fooled! It is a selfish act, to serve the ego by seemingly becoming egoless. The approach towards life is down to the individual. You might say that life is hard and full of problems or you look at it as a challenge that provides you with unsolved tasks to learn from.

There is another common group of earthlings: the consumerists. They only believe in what they see – which is obviously very limited – and they build their material wealth, indulge the physical body and go through their chosen experiences in life. This group of earthlings are connected to Earth element. Sometimes they hit Water and very seldom arrives at the level of Air. Fire definitely avoids this group.

If I had to classify the 2 approaches I would definitely vote for the latter. They work, they use their brains and they even exercise their physical body and look after it. They also play with emotions and one day they might just wake up with the desire to change! To reach the macrocosmic Fire element from Earth through Water and Air as the major stations of evolution is a strong possibility. On the other hand, reaching for the macrocosm without understanding the micro is a definite naïve choice and shift of responsibilities.

Every human relationship is based upon the evolutionary state of the self. In interrelations individuals should learn each other through unconditional trust and love. This type of love is helpful and emotionless; the secret of which is to understand the fact that earthlings perform the 100% of their abilities at every given time. It is only expectation that belittles it.

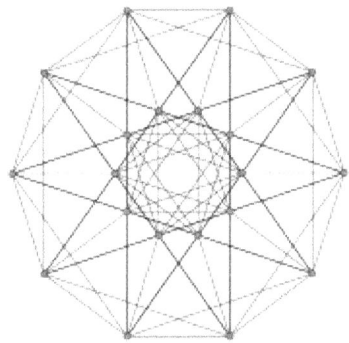

AKIA PHILOSOPHY®

HEALER LEVEL

WATER INITIATION

2

- **Astral travelling and meditation**

As you remember, every earthling has an astral body. Even those, without the past knowledge of the soul are able to take on travelling tasks in the universe. These journeys are either consciously designed by the earthling or could be a *call* from the universe in order to further the soul on its evolutionary task. Robot-like earthlings receive their duties from the code given to them by a higher power. They are used by the power to advance its desire rather than the Self for self doesn't exist without soul. Our teachings embrace spiritual learning and deals with the soul as the necessary requirement to the process.

The astral body is a straight connection to the macrocosm that keeps you informed of the changes and brings ideas from different planes to help your earthly life. Dreams you receive during various cycles of resting, intuition, some of the so-called illusions and fantasies arrive by the help of it. Every meditation is an astral travelling regardless of the length, depth and purpose. A simple closed eyes *Om* chanting would take you out there, just as a conscious religious prayer. It is natural, for you do it as you build a bridge, connect and convey wishes, requests or admiration to a power out there.

All souls, regardless of the place of existence, are connected to the Creator Force. It is the origin of every organic energy and the centre of the great matrix of the Universe. When we talk about creation it is not limited to earthlings or other souls but embraces everything: planets, rocks, stars, animals and vegetation; all the chemical substances around and out there.

I cannot emphasize enough, that souls on earth need the three bodies to survive. The physical body ensures the physical nourishment and reproduction of such bodies; the astral body is the straight way to the Source and the spiritual is the connection between the two. The soul blends into those bodies so all 3 of them is the soul on a different plane. They are interrelated but able to perform certain task by themselves. The astral body is the head of the soul, the spiritual is the neck of it and the physical body represents the earthly, material connection needed to the survival of the earthling. Therefore, when the astral body goes out there, it also endangers the soul. Without adequate protection a seemingly innocent meditation could badly backfire.

Every meditation needs a purpose. It is not enough to empty yourself or become nothing as the fashionable surface-Buddhism is teaching to the eager – to – survive, overstressed and lost European and North-American population, but fill up this void with something useful. Chanting *Love, World Peace* and *Feed the Poor* only satisfies the ego and hardly produces changes on the subject. The great paradox is that those teachings denounce the ego as an unnecessary bad, and might not realize that they actually boost the ego and put the soul into latency. However, the ego cannot be eliminated. It represents the element of Earth in the mind, without which the life of an earthling is not complete.

The real work starts at home by understanding the reasons behind events and by realizing that you are responsible for the happenings on Earth.

- **The Merkaba**

Every soul in the Universe has at least one Merkaba. It is a spaceship that helps the journeys of the soul and provides basic protection. Having said that, it doesn't mean that your Merkaba is always with you regardless and no harm can come to your astral body. One needs to use it consciously and purposefully very much like a car.

It is time for you to find and start using your own personal Merkaba. In order to do it you start up with golden light from the Universe and create the yellow brick road. Start walking on it until you notice a parking lot where are spaceship-like vehicles wait for the rightful owners to pick them up. Follow your intuition and choose the one you feel close to. Go to the door and put your thumb on the doorknob. If it opens you are at home. If not, you continue searching. You might get chased by rightful owners who get suspicious of your lurking around. Just explain your task and everything will be all right.

As the door opens you find yourself in a circular space with few chairs and a dashboard in front of you. There is a built-in cupboard on your right. The place is dusty and neglected, waiting for you to give it thorough cleaning. You find materials in the cupboard. Please, control your curiosity and do not push any buttons! All to be learnt! The only thing you need to know is the driver's seat and the stick on the left if you are left-handed, and on the right, if you favour the right hand. Pushing it forward and announcing the destination, the Merkaba will take you there.

When you finished, leave the place and close the door behind. Turn your head as you walk away and notice a clear 3 – 4-digit number on the side of your Merkaba. The 4-digit should start with 11, 12, 13, 14 or 15. However the 3 digits cannot start with 1. Make note of this number and submit with your other exercises, for I need to make sure you arrived to the right one. Walk back on the road and finish as always.

- **The 22-star formations zodiac**

As I have mentioned earlier, with the Quantum Leap we arrived back to the zodiac of the 22-star formations. Arriving back somewhere is only a figure of speech. The expression was created during the Neptune – Pisces era when places and earthlings were looked at as static with permanent data and knowledge attached. The pre-destined life provided very narrow leeway, therefore looking at life as unchangeable became a favoured view point on Keta. In reality we can never go back to where we have been and nothing will ever be as it was. During the 16,000 years we have evolved so did the mentioned zodiac. Nevertheless, we are here and excitingly waiting for new influences from each other.

Everything in the Universe, even letters, is made up of numbers. However, there are only ten significant numbers and 22 letters. Each of these letters as a symbol, provides an important energy structure. Although out of all the alphabets we might know, Latin letters are the youngest, I chose them because I am writing on a language using the same symbols. It is no point translating them into other structures because they carry different energies. It means that as energy the letter "A" might correspond with "S" in another alphabet.

Each one of the star formations represent the energy of a certain letter.

It the following train of exercises and astral travelling you have to become the particular letter as it is drawn.

I number every star-formations we are working with in order to provide the safest and the best place for experiences needed. To help you with the experiment I added some naturalistic of the letter in question.

Let us start with letter A. On the way to your Merkaba you imagine that you are this particular symbol as it is drawn. In addition, you feel that your colour is changing into light blue and you resonate high. Air element would lift you from the ground. You'll do the same with all the letters given. I suggest you do no more than 3 travels in one go. Each time you need to get ready for the journey by doing the 2 meditations below to be properly cleansed and filled with light.

BEADBOARD MEDITATION

The meditation – The Beadboard

VISIT THE SUN MEDITATION

The meditation- Visit the Sun

Note

Please do not forget to write your experiences in your journal.

BECOME A LETTER MEDITATION

The meditation – Become a letter

Note

Each time you set off for a different planet you need to do the light catching from the Universe and the projection to form the yellow brick road that leads you to your merkaba. Use the formation and the number given for your destination. On arrival to the planet, you introduce yourself and state that you learning AKIA. Listen to your intuition and take the personal messages you are given. On one of the planets, you will receive a name. Write it down. Then come back to Earth, take the road back and release the light thanking. After you make note of the experience and thoughts came to you during the journey.

ORION – LETTER A

Orion 13

It is light blue in colour with high resonance; belongs to Air element.

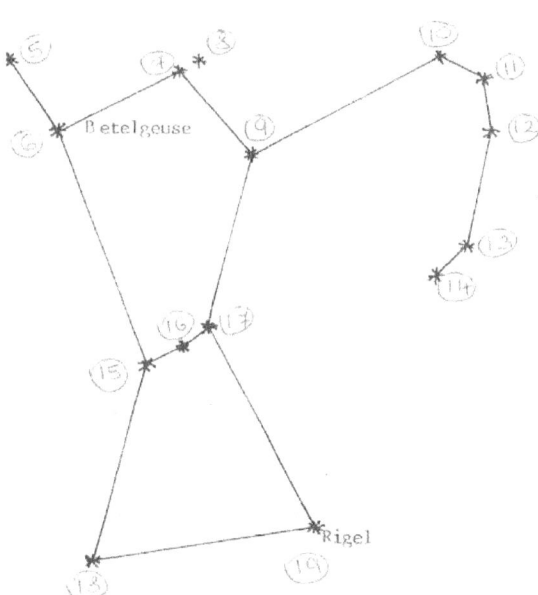

Wise Centaur 8

It is light violet in colour with high resonance; belongs to Water element.

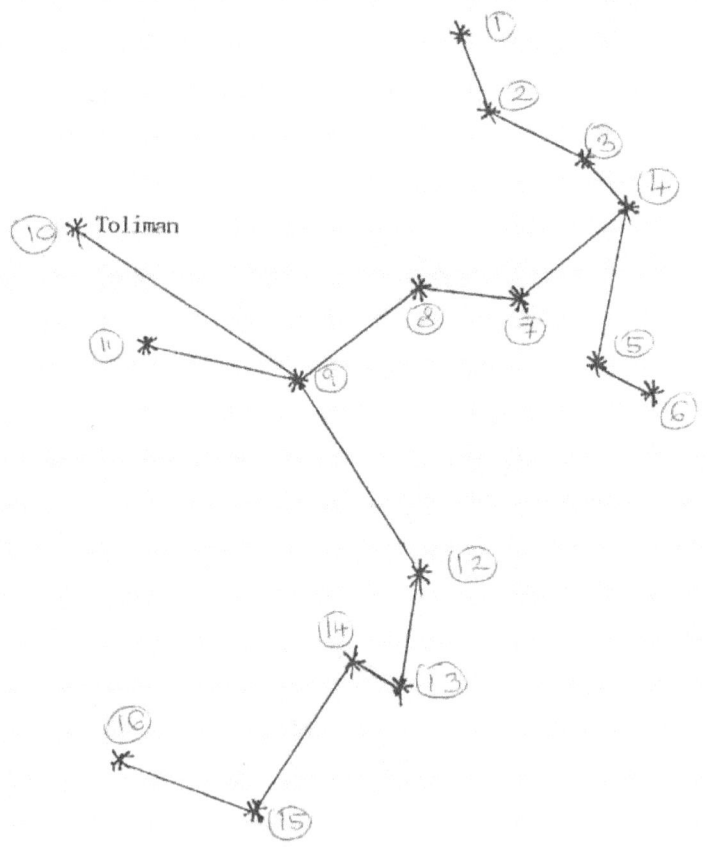

Raven 2

It is vermilion in colour with moderate resonance; belongs to Fire element.

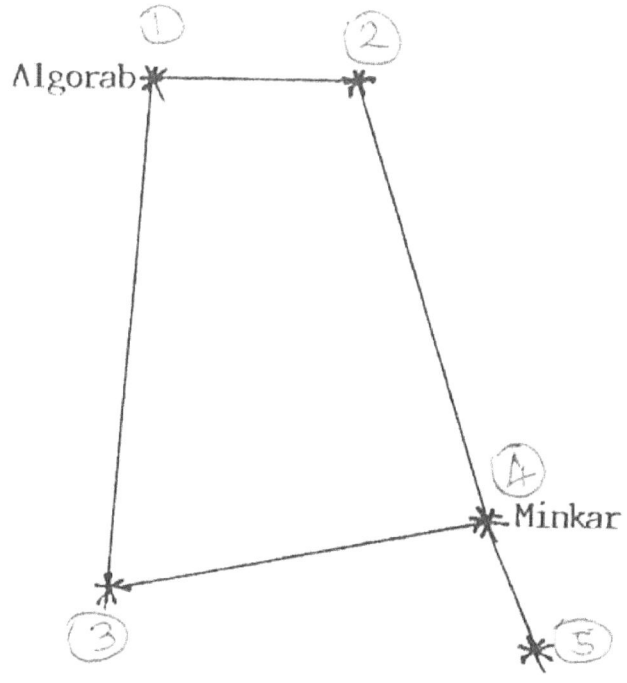

ANDROMEDA – LETTER D

Andromeda 4

It is dark blue in colour with low resonance; belongs to Earth element.

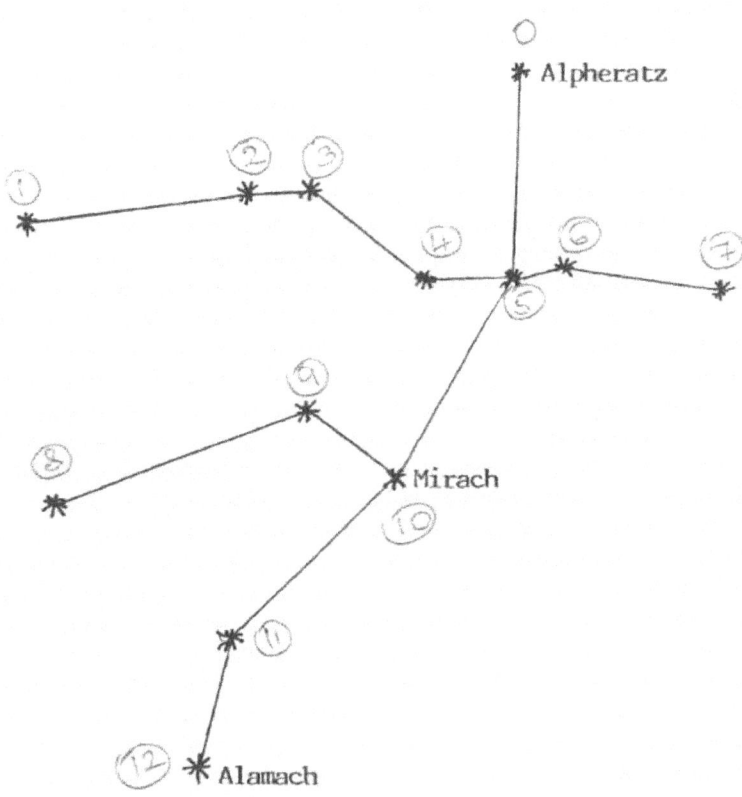

CROWN OF THE NORTH WIND – LETTER E

Crown of the North Wind 4

It is dark violet in colour with low resonance; belongs to Fire element.

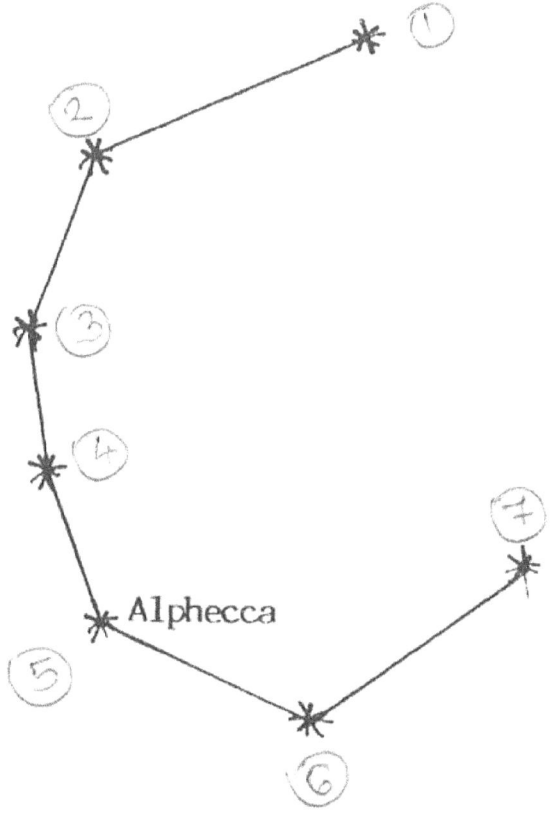

PERSEUS – LETTER F

Perseus 5

It is light green in colour with high resonance; belongs to Water element.

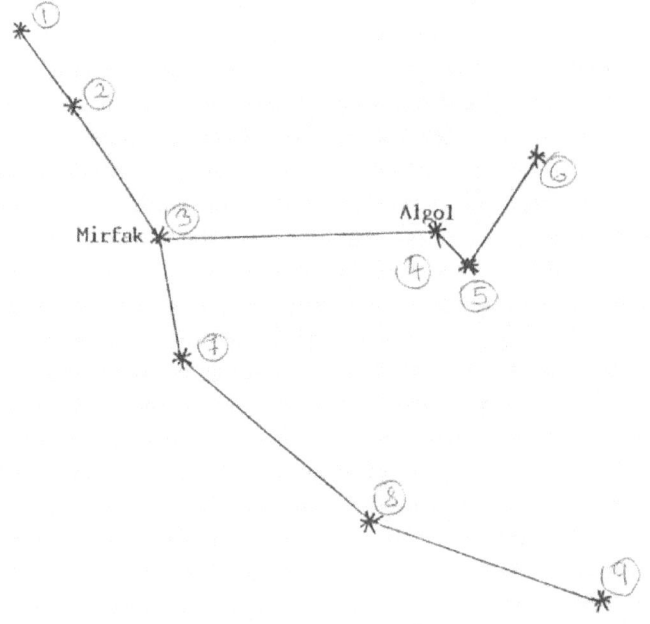

THE RIVER OF THE NIGHT – LETTER G

The River of the Night - Eridanus 13

It is grass green in colour with moderate to low resonance; belongs to Earth element.

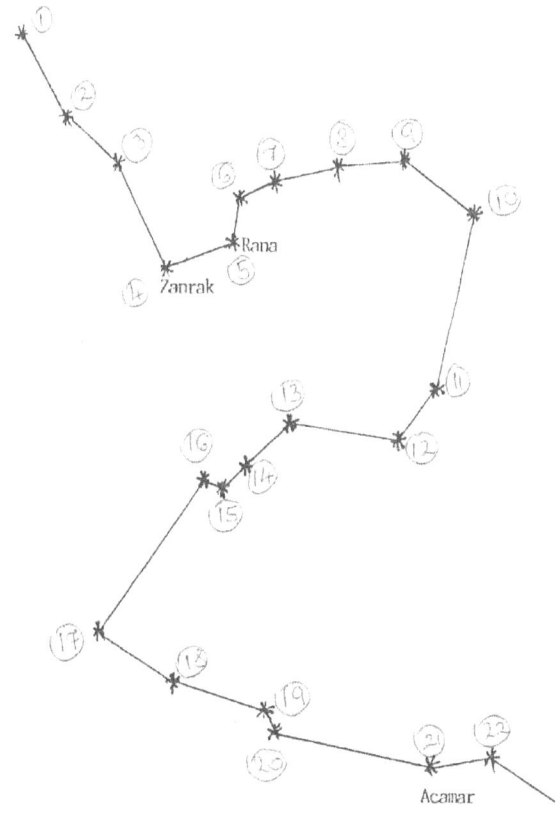

PEGASUS – LETTER H

Pegasus 5

It is silver-violet in colour with high resonance; belongs to Water element.

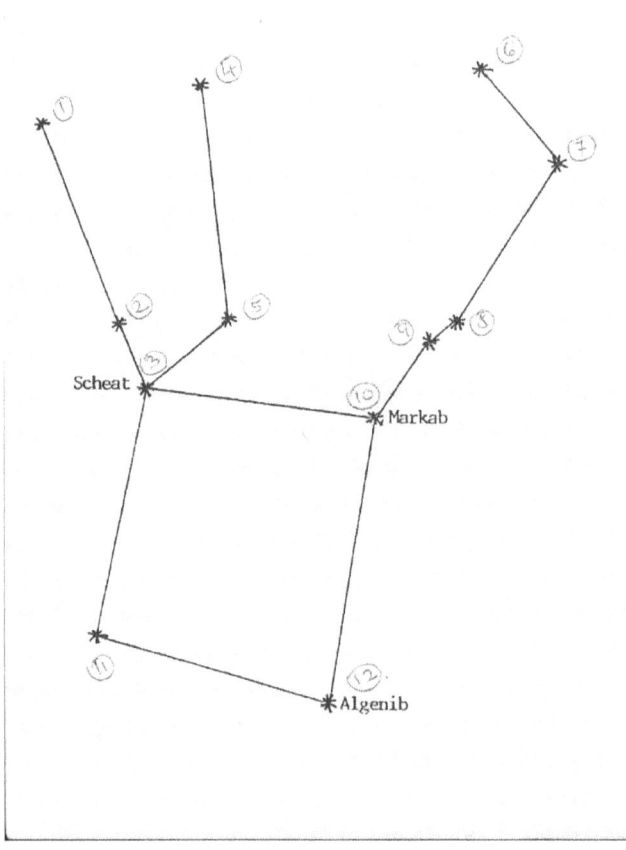

LYRA – LETTER Y

Lyra of Orpheus 1

It is light opal in colour with high resonance; belongs to Earth element.

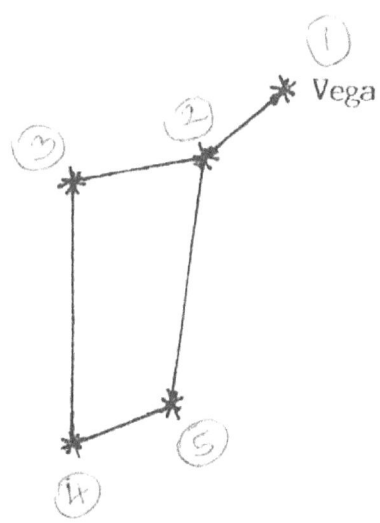

DOLPHIN – LETTER J

Dolphin 2

It is opal in colour with moderate resonance; belongs to Earth element.

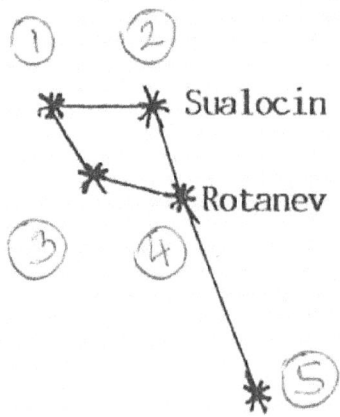

OPHIUCUS – LETTER K

Ophiucus – The serpent bearer 3

It is silvery blue in colour with high resonance; belongs to Air and Fire elements.

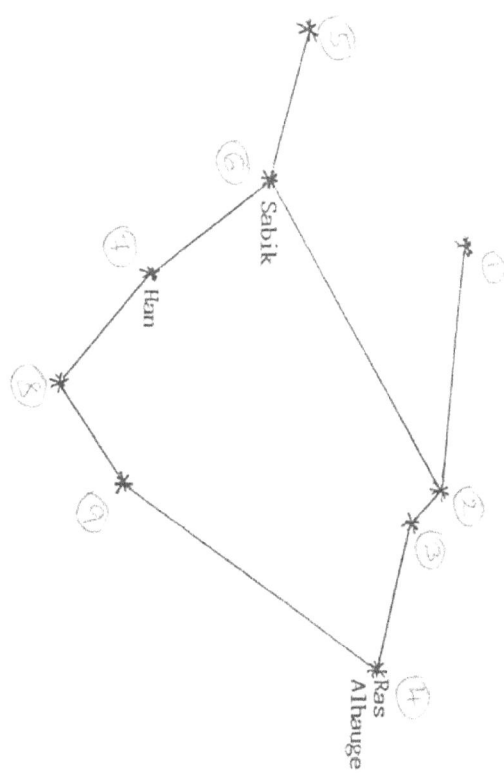

URSA MAJOR – LETTER L

The Great Bear - Ursa Major 4

It is dark green in colour with low resonance; belongs to Air element.

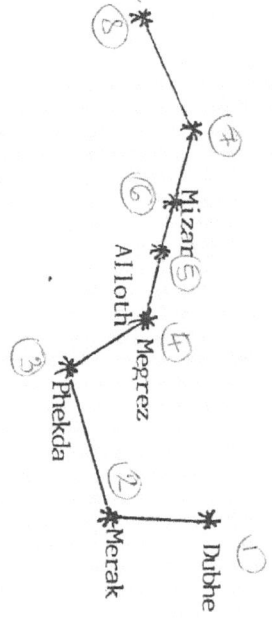

DRACO – LETTER M

Dragon - Draco 12

It is sea-green in colour with moderate resonance; belongs to Water element.

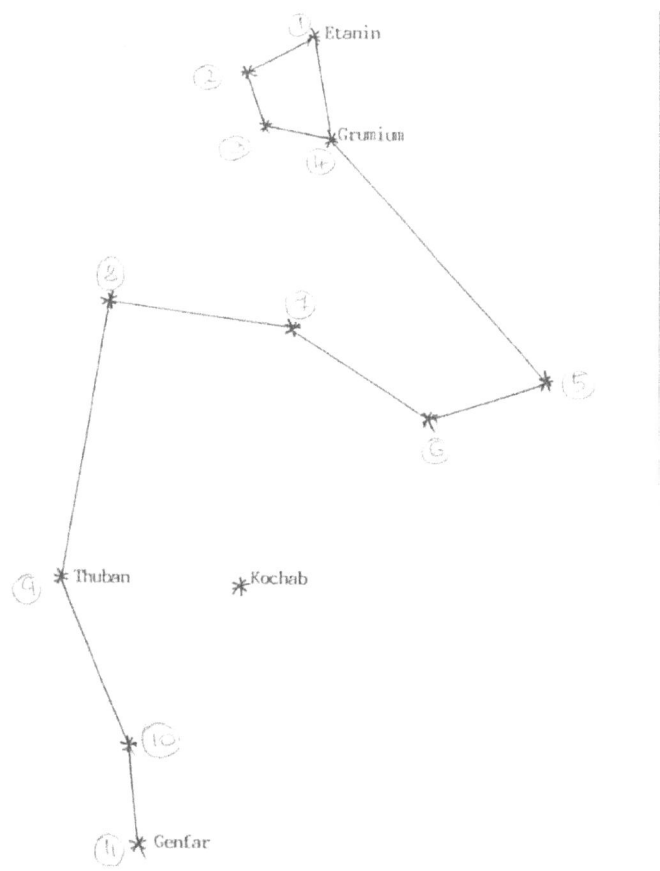

SERPENT – LETTER N

Serpent 4

It is red in colour with low resonance; belongs to Fire element.

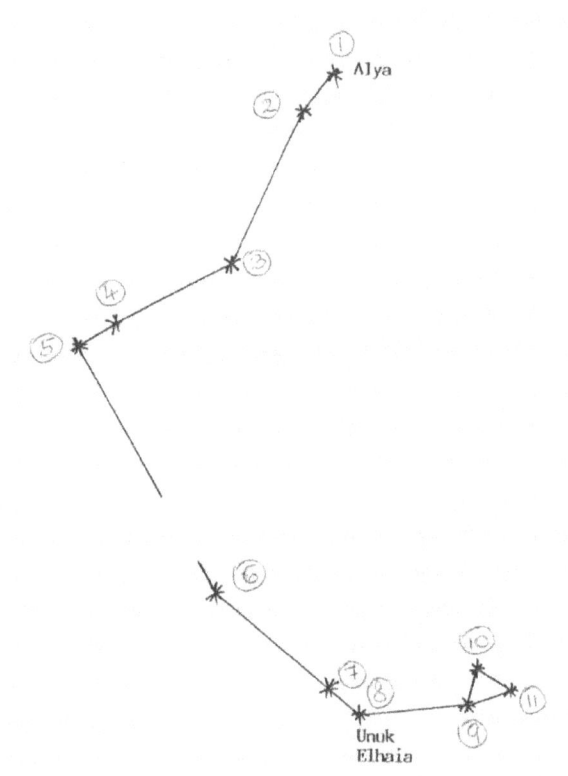

SEA SERPENT – LETTER O

Sea Serpent 14

It is deep-blue in colour with low resonance; belongs to Water element.

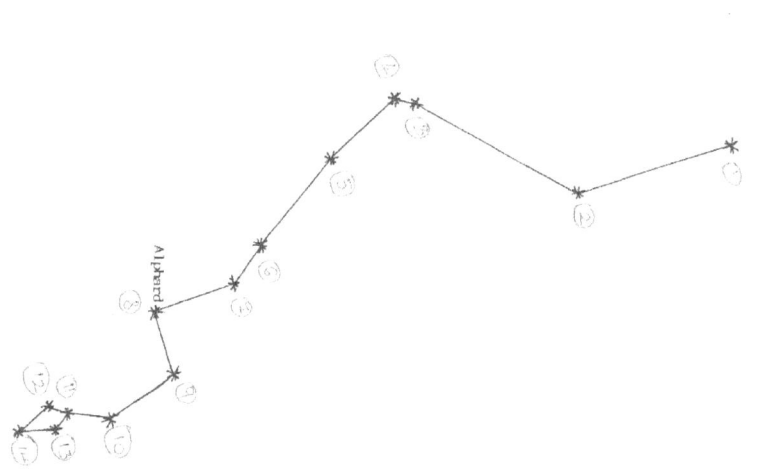

CANIS MAJOR, CANIS MINOR – LETTER P

Dogs - Canis Major 12

It is dark-grey in colour with very low resonance; belongs to Earth element.

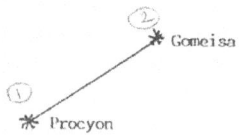

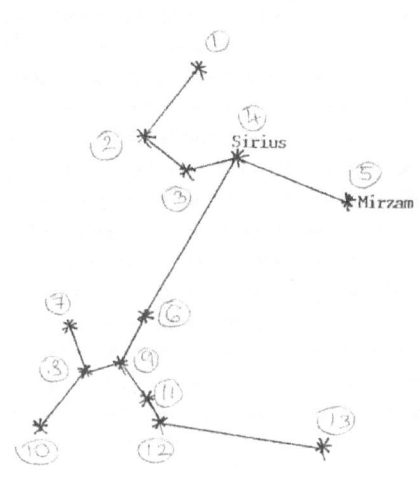

THE CUP – LETTER R

Cup 2

Brilliant-golden in colour with high resonance; belongs to Water element.

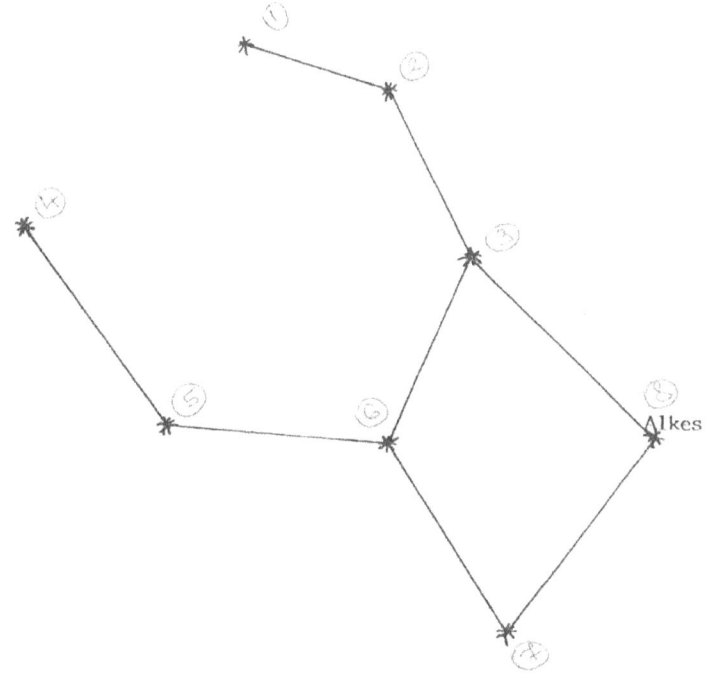

THE CHARIOTEER – LETTER S

Charioteer 3

It is crimson in colour with moderate resonance; belongs to Fire element.

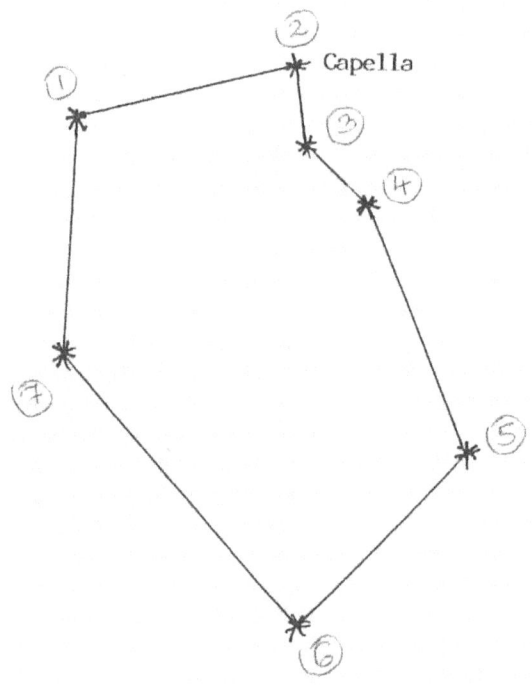

SHIP OF THE ARGONAUTS – LETTER T

Ship of the Argonauts 7

It is brownish-black in colour with low resonance; belongs to Earth element.

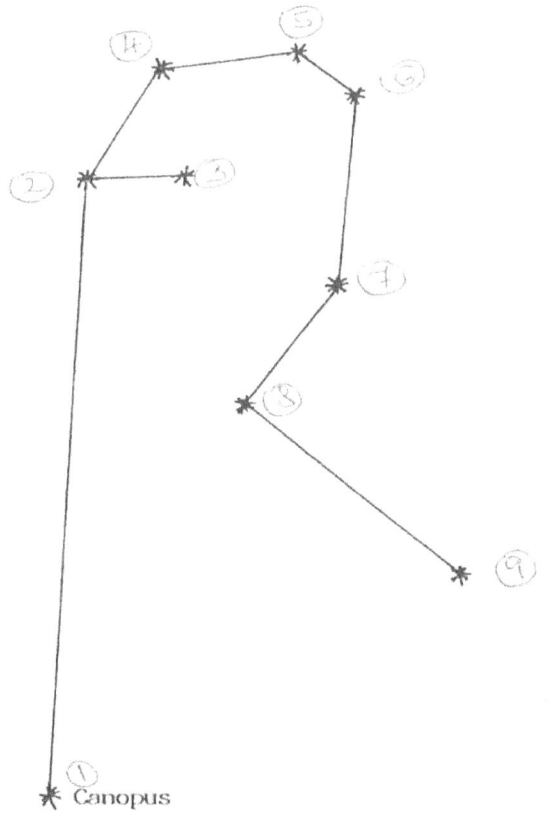

AGUILA – LETTER U

Aquila - Eagle 5

It is velvet-black in colour with low resonance; belongs to Earth and Air elements.

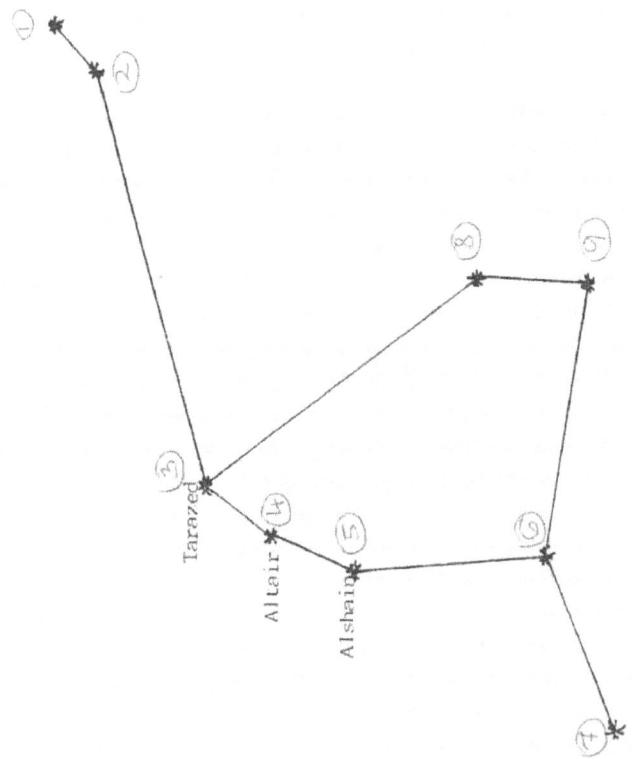

THE SWAN – LETTER V

Swan 8

It is light green in colour with high resonance; belongs to Water element.

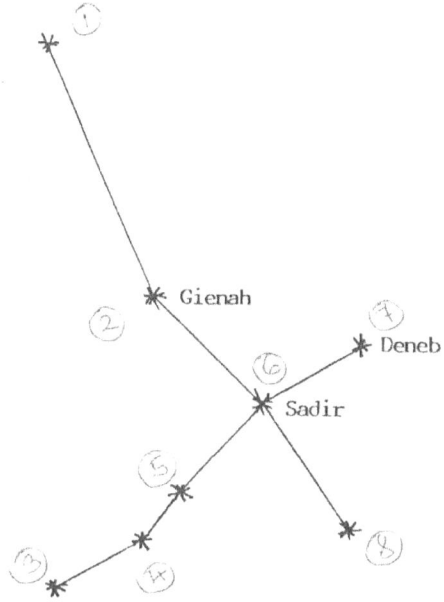

THE BEAR KEEPER – LETTER Z

Bear Keeper 15

It is indigo in colour with high resonance; belongs to Fire element.

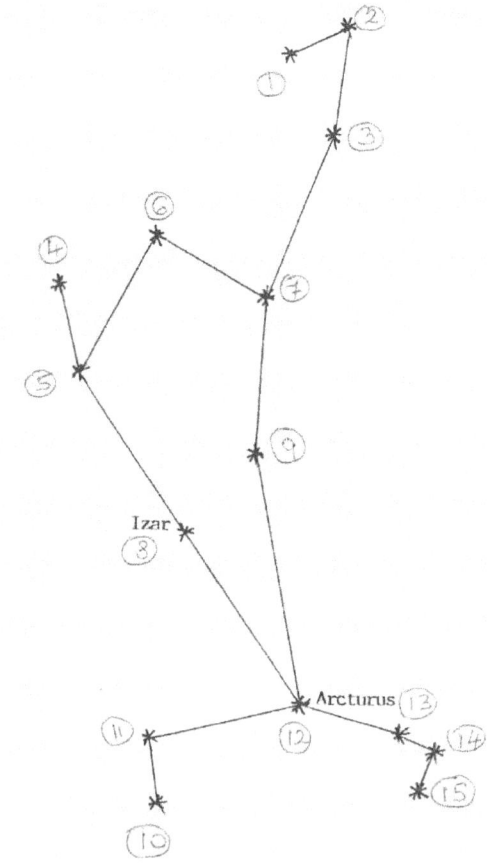

Practice

This is one of the most exciting and amazing experience one can go through. Let your imagination run wild and do not be afraid of anything facing you. You never receive larger task than your capabilities, so dig in and find the courage within. I am always there to keep eye on you.

Experience the real and unlimited freedom: the freedom of thoughts.

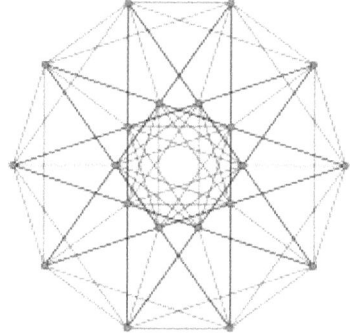

AKIAPHILOSOPHY®

HEALER LEVEL

WATER INITIATION

3

BEADBOARD MEDITATION

The meditation – The Beadboard

THANKSGIVING MEDITATION

The meditation – Thanksgiving

- **Symbols**

Symbols are certain forms and drawings designated to particular philosophies, religions or ideas. Everything that carries hidden value is considered to belong to this category.

Due to its nature the meaning of a certain symbol is only clear to the origin; being it a group or an individual. Outsiders need to dig and familiarize with the thought behind. Even in this case a symbol might be misunderstood down to the filter of the investigator.

Let us look at one of the most commonly used symbols, the five-pointed star.

 Here is the five-pointed star used for Occult Knowledge. In this shape it is called the pentagram. It depicts the Magick capabilities of Earthlings, usually attributed to the chosen ones and prohibited by certain religions.

In magick works, like witchcraft and other Shamanic practices the pentagram is drawn to strengthen rituals and healing work.

It is usually white in colour with black background.

 In this form the five-pointed star usually means Communism. It has been adopted for the political and commercial structure because of the original meaning of New, Strong and Change. The colour red is Fire.

Although today most people would turn away from the idea of Communism; however, it is interesting to see China as the major lender of the U.S.A.

The upside-down pentagram usually symbolises the Devil in the form of the Himalayan goat. The quaint smile on his face talks about earthly pleasures. The 2 names would clearly classify this joy as sexual.

Not many earthlings know that in the Old Testament Adam's wife was Lilith. However, she tasted the apple – that is the symbol of Knowledge – and decided to go through the experiences of existence with Hades in the Underworld. Samael follows the Hebrew understanding of the latter.

Lilith received condemnation and Adam was rewarded a wife of purity, without sexual desires who he created from his rib.

It is also interesting to know that this symbol, on its own right without the writings, originally depicted Life with its pleasures and sorrows. Devil was created at a much later stage to keep people back for learning.

We all know this symbol. It depicts the life of an earthling through learning and understanding the 4 elements and finding its place in the cycle of nature to become the part of the Great Matrix. When it happens, the earthling connects to the Creator force, represented by the fifth point, the head.

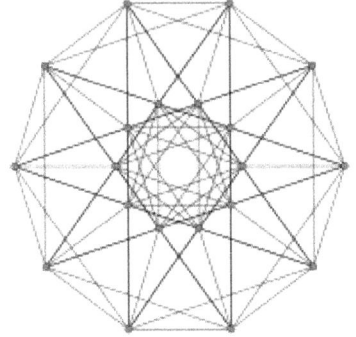

This drawing is to show how very perfect a pentagram is!

Every meaningful symbol is in this picture.

Again it is an upside-down pentagram, usually representing secret societies with dark or hidden aims and practices.

As you can see the centre is a perfect Pentagon…

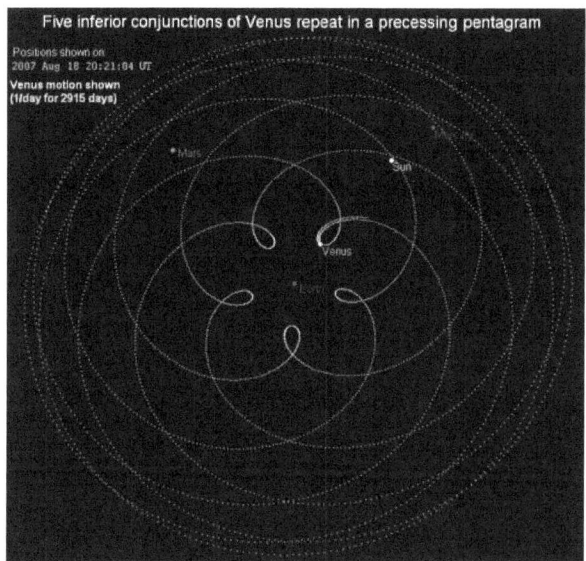

And this is the journey of Venus where the five-pointed star originates from. She opened channels for us to connect to the macrocosm and embrace the Occult Knowledge.

Venus is curious, unpredictable and strong. She is the perfect female with her healing power and motherly care, constantly there, guiding us. She is the great lover with divine knowledge and passion, who never stops evolving.

Practice

As you walk find 20 symbols and explain them according to your understanding. They might be in logos, stonework, on clothing or in media.

- **Handling criticism**

Earthlings are not very comfortable when it comes to handling criticism. It derives from ideas and preconceptions about behaviour patterns and the widely accepted good and bad.

Practice

I would like you to write down the 10 most common criticism that arrive at you from fellow beings. How do you handle them? What kind of emotions they trigger in you? Do you treat criticism differently from friends, family members? Why?

WATER MEDITATION

The meditation – water

Sit down on the floor with straight back. Open your knees as much as you can. Your arms on your side or on your knees, comfortably.
Relax.
Open your crown chakra, that is above your head and take a slow and deep breath. Down into the diaphragm.
Imagine that the energy above your head becomes a thick silver prism of light. As you breathe in the prism reaches the end of your spine, the Root chakra at the caudal vertebra to create a wonderfully glowing cleansing and healing connection between your energy centres. Slowly release the air from your lung. As you do it slowly, feel the oxygen reaching even the smallest corner of your body making you feel hot. One-two-three-in and one-two-three-out. One-two-three-in and one-two-three-out.

Keeping the breathing rhythm, crouch with your head at the knees, imitating a drop of water. Then stand up and stretch, try to reach the sky. Crouch again and stretch. As you repeat the motion few times, you feel the sensation of growing. Your belly grows, your chest and your buttocks. The movements get slower and the drop longer. You cannot hold it together anymore. The drop starts its journey. Gathers the smaller drops on the way. Waters the trees, offers drink to the birds and caresses the bathing animals.

Grows and grows, running on the road faster and faster. Gets wider and deeper, searching for a safe channel. Washes away the dirt and the trees, move the rocks.

The Sun comes up. Playfully caresses the water, dances on the waves. The exercise makes him thirsty. Drinks from the water and continue the movement. The beams want more and more water. The dance fastens and you get smaller. Animals cannot drink from you anymore. You are stranded. Every move hurts. Crouch and offer yourself to the Universe.

Send back the silver energy, thank for it and come back to your earthly existence.

AKIA PHILOSOPHY®

HEALER LEVEL

WATER INITIATION

4

Prepare for initiation

Here we are again, at the second initiation. You have come a long way; covered miles of information, done hours of exercises and dug into your soul deeply. You can cleanse your body, help others doing it, able to ride a merkaba and travel in the Universe. Are you confused? I am certain you are! It is all right. We all are from time to time. The benefits of this initiation will come to you at a later stage. I do not mean years but it definitely takes some time to sink in and to blend into the way of living.

Hopefully it will alter the filter through which you look at others and the way you think others look at you. Don't forget! There are lot of assumptions, preconceptions and theatrical plays to clear if you attempt to find yourself. Remember, all earthlings go through the same struggle. Be patient and offer your unconditional love.

BEADBOARD MEDITATION

The meditation – The Beadboard

VISIT THE SUN MEDITATION

The meditation – Visit the Sun

VISIT YOUR SPIRIT GUIDE MEDITATION

The meditation – Visit your spirit guides in your Temple

Note

Everything you experience, learn or see during meditations needs to be added to your notes in the **Journal of Journeys.**

Reminder

AKIA is the philosophy of The Unseen Soul and Cosmic Knowledge, therefore, the task is to make it accessible for everybody. At this moment we only have the material in English but I am constantly looking for prospective teachers and colleagues with different mother tongue who could translate our teachings.

Initiations usually work centrally when we meet at a given time and I could initiate or you might say attune you with the element of Earth. On the day of initiation, you cleanse yourself and say the AKIA mantra 13 times. Wear white clothing and build a channel with your logo.

Connect with your teacher online who would say the initiation mantra up front that you need to repeat and add your name when applicable. When finished I would personally attune you.

Note

We organize initiation rituals online twice a year.

MANTRA OF THE 2nd INITIATION OF THE UNIVERSE

I ... solemnly promise that the knowledge I gained

I will only use according to the Laws of the Universe.

I clear my thoughts regularly.

I trust the Universe and myself.

Doubts have no place in my life.

Thanks for your trust in me,

That I will always treasure.

Thank you for Blessing me.

Note

Apart from the Old and New Testaments God by any names always mean the Universe. It is the Higher Force, the Laws of Life, the Quintessence and the First Knowledge that was able to multiply by division. However, with AKIA you need to open your horizon and go beyond religious views for you are on the path to find yourself and not a religion.

This path is rockier but much more rewarding. You'll gain a vast amount of information and arrive at understand more and more interrelations of events. You'll lose your fear and develop great respect for Life; one day you'll realize that you need to bear responsibility for your deeds, words and thoughts because you are a co-creator.

I hope you enjoyed my book. In case you wish to know more you might refer to the https://ex-files.org site or come to our live and online webinars. Alternatively wait for the next book on the gnostic knowledge of AKIA Philosophy®.

I wish you well.

https://zsazsatudos.com/

zsazsa@zsazsatudos.com

www.ingramcontent.com/pod-product-compliance
Lightning Source LLC
Chambersburg PA
CBHW060758110426
42739CB00033BA/3211